VOICES FROM NORTH-EAST INDIA

NAGA LAND

Deutscher Kunstverlag

HUMBOLDT FORUM

CONTENTS

FOREWORD

Hartmut Dorgerloh and Lars-Christian Koch

Tradition and *identity*, often mentioned in one breath, seem to constitute an interdependent concept pair. Yet, (why) is this the case? What is hidden behind a 'tradition'? A cultural guide pattern? A construct – mutable or unvarying? And what exactly does 'identity' mean? 'Being the same'? How many identities can there be, how large or small in scope can they be, how changeable are they and how formative for the way an individual, a family, a group, a quite large community or a state view themselves culturally and societally?

'This is a question I'm still grappling with, because I cannot define what identity is, because for me it's so fluid,' says Zubeni Lotha, art historian and art photographer from Dimapur, who has co-curated the exhibition *Naga Land: Voices from North-east India* with Roland Platz, curator at the Berlin Ethnological Museum. 'I don't know what being a Naga means. ... Because I don't know what a Naga is supposed to behave like, act like, look like, eat, walk sleep.'[1] Against the background of her personal identity as a Na-ga, she goes into the question of who the Naga are and how a presumably collective Naga culture is expressed.

Seven hundred and fifty *scheduled tribes* are recorded as living in India, which amounts to about 8.6 percent of the overall population. These indigenous societies belong to a variety of different ethnic groups, live in settlement areas that are separated from each other, all with languages, cultures and social structures of their own, as is the case of the Tibeto-Burman Naga group in the north-east – three to four million people, who live in Nagaland and in the abutting Indian states as well as Myanmar. Nor are they a homogeneous indigenous minority; quite the contrary, they fall into more than thirty groups, each with its own language and dialects. For all their differences, these local identities are linked by a primary consciousness of being Naga. This awareness is expressed in their material culture, in performances and observances and the pursuit of common political goals. But what exactly is its essence? ———

In the days of India's colonial dependency, drawn borders reinforced cultural and political differences and isolated the Naga settlement area as well: the introduction of an *inner line* through the area under British administration in 1873 made entering and leaving this mountainous region more difficult. Synchronously the autonomous Naga villages came under the sway of North American Baptist missionaries. Taking harsh measures to suppress local animist thinking and rituals, they converted the Naga to Christianity. About 90 percent of the state's population are now Christians rather than Hindus. Arousing awareness of traditions and an identity the state's inhabitants have in common also entails demarcation from what recognisably does not belong and defining what does. ———

The idea of a linking Naga identity became the driving force behind movements for political autonomy. Incorporation of the Naga settlement area in the nation state while India was in the process of achieving independence increased Naga resistance from 1947 and sparked armed struggles for independence from the Indian centralised government. As a concession to the Naga the state of Nagaland was created in 1963 along with the promise of a large degree of autonomy. ———

Against that backdrop, studying one of Europe's earliest and most extensive historical collections of objects and artefacts from Naga cultures leads to the core of a link between identity and tradition. The Ethnologisches Museum Berlin collection comprises some 1,300 Naga objects: textiles, jewellery, utensils and weapons as well as historic photographs, which no one in Nagaland knew existed until 2014.[2] Even now the exact circumstances under which they were acquired remain for the most part unclarified. The first collection of objects was assembled in 1878 by Adolf Bastian, founding director of the Museum für Völkerkunde, on his return to Berlin from travels in the region. Those historical artefacts bridge past and present in *Naga Land: Voices from North-east India*. Since 2015, we have been looking through them for the exhibition jointly with representatives of the Naga; the exhibits have been researched and confronted with contemporary artefacts. Bringing forms to life by so vividly reviving and recreating them memorably reveals the mutability and diversity of tradition and identity, which, at once impoverishment and enrichment, possess the potential for reinventing the past and sustainably shaping future developments. ———

Naga Land: Voices from North-east India is an interdisciplinary exhibition that has been organised as a collective project involving curators at the Berlin Ethnological Museum and the Humboldt Forum Foundation in the Berlin Palace together with Zubeni Lotha, artist and co-curator. Our warmest thanks to all those who have collaborated on all stages of this undertaking.

1 Quotation translated by L. Goldenbaum. Zubeni Lotha, in 'The Hutton Lectures', Kohima Institute, Nagaland, 3 December 2014. Many thanks to Michael Heneise for this reference. Quoted in: Marion Wettstein, 'How Ethnic Identity Becomes Real: The Enactment of Identity Roles and the Material Manifestation of Shifting Identities Among the Nagas', *Asian Ethnicity* 17, no. 3 (201): 384–399, here 384.

2 'Nagaland Connections – Zum Aufbau einer Kooperation zwischen dem Ethnologischen Museum Berlin und Angehörigen der Naga-Community', in *Baessler-Archiv*, 2018/19, Vol. 65, pp. 197–202.

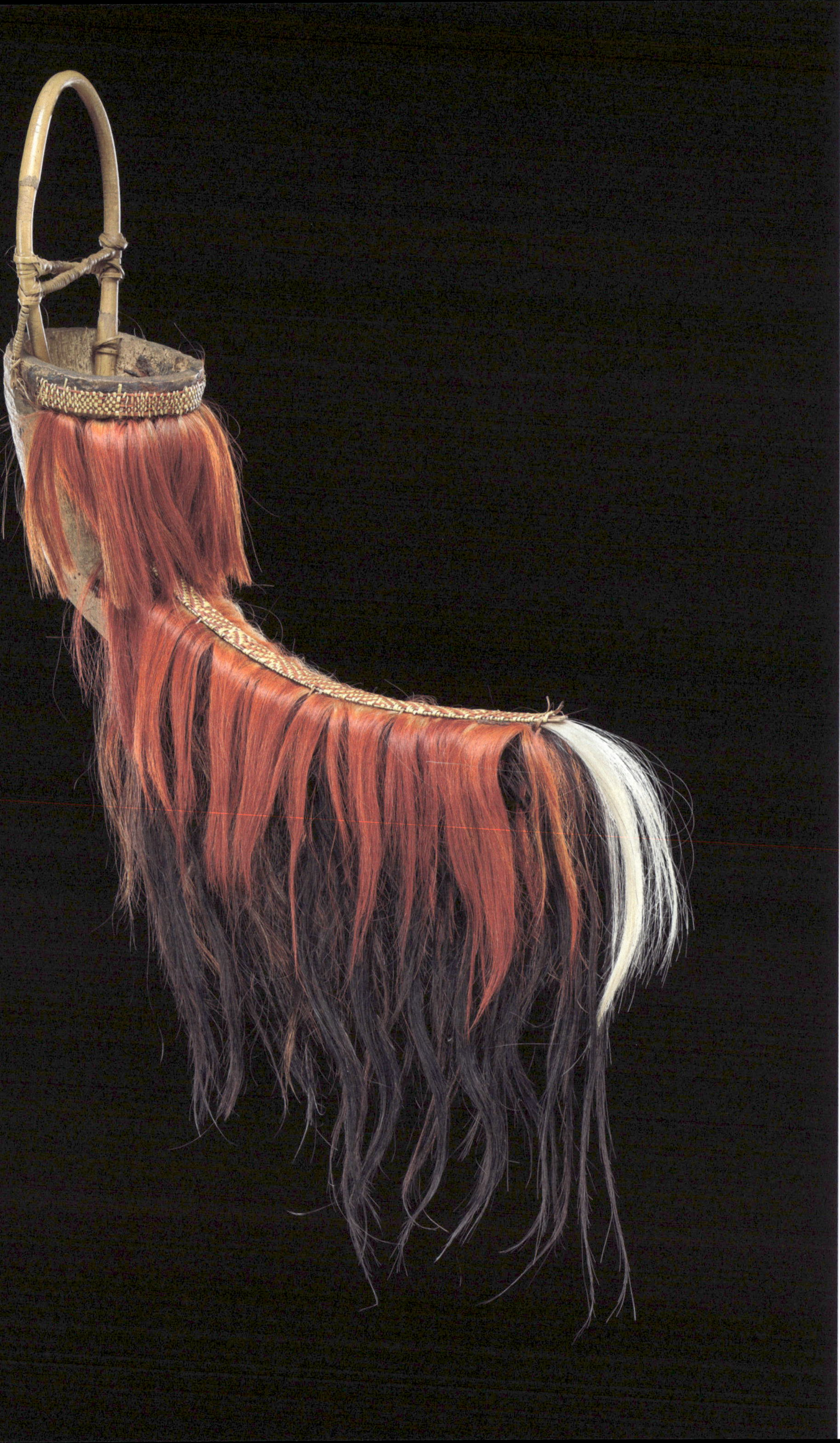

INTRODUCTION

Roland Platz

This book is published to accompany *Naga Land: Voices from North-east India*, an exhibition at the Berlin Humboldt Forum. It covers, or goes deeper into, subjects for which there was no space at the exhibition, or which could only be briefly touched on. ———

The exhibition is a collaborative project shared by a team of German curators and a curator from Nagaland. Thematically, the project deals with the question of whether there is an identity all Naga have in common and the role their material culture and socio-cultural traditions play in such an identity. The Naga, representative of many other minorities in South and South-east Asia, attempt to demarcate themselves from the Indian social majority even though they also form part of it. Yet, who are the Naga in fact? ———

The Naga consist of more than thirty ethnic groups. They all belong to the Tibeto-Burman language family but for the most part do not understand each other's individual languages. Along with English, Nagamese has become the lingua franca among them. Nagamese is a composite language made up of Assamese, Bengali, Nepali and English. All Naga groups are traditionally acephalous societies, that is, societies lacking centralised state structures. Some writers on the subjects also speak of 'village republics' in this connection.[1] Most Naga settlements are relatively large, comprising at least one hundred households, and are organised by clans, each of which lives in a particular part of a village (*khel*). Before the advent of the British, ethnicity was far less important: clan, village and familial affiliations mattered far more then.[2] However, ethnicity has become a major identity marker. This is shown by the way the Naga settle by ethnicity in the larger cities of the region nowadays.

Fig. 1 Panji basket with tail (*shi shuku*), Ao Naga, Nagaland, latter half 19th century, bamboo, rattan, stained and dyed hair
Otto E. Ehlers Collection, donated in 1896 to the Royal Museum of Ethnology, Inv. No. IC28472, Staatliche Museen zu Berlin, Ethnologisches Museum

All Naga groups sporadically practised headhunting well into the twentieth century. Headhunting was not so much a religious component of Naga culture but a social one that served primarily to enhance prestige.[3] The Naga traditionally practised slash-and-burn agriculture[4] (*jum*) with swidden fields of mountain rice, their most important crop, later followed also by rice grown in paddy fields in areas suitable for semiaquatic growing conditions. The settlement area of the three to four million Naga stretches across north-east India to include the modern Indian states of Nagaland, Assam, Arunachal Pradesh and Manipur as well as part of north-western Myanmar. The Naga constitute the majority population only in the state of Nagaland. 'Naga' is a self-definition that has political connotations and is used flexibly. Hence the population count varies for the Naga, linked with constantly changing group names and alliances. ———

The colonial and post-colonial history of the Naga is a history of resistance, which was directed primarily against the Indian government after India became independent in 1947. It should be borne in mind that the Naga had already fought battles against the British? in the nineteenth century. Between 1835 and 1855 alone there were ten British 'punitive expeditions', as they were known, which resulted in villages being burnt down.[5] In the twentieth century, too, military operations were still sporadically targeting Naga groups who, in defiance of the British ban on headhunting, continued to practise it. Nonetheless the Naga managed to retain a certain degree of autonomy in the colonial era in line with the British *divide et impera* strategy. At the same time, there was quite a large region designated an 'unadministered area'. It stretched along what is now the border with Myanmar, and the British never succeeded in bringing it under control. In the 1950s, the Naga began to engage in armed conflict with the Indian government that raged most fiercely in the 1970s and 1980s. Moreover, in the 1990s, fighting between rival Naga groups flared up with increasing frequency.[6] Since the armistice agreed in 1997 between the Indian government

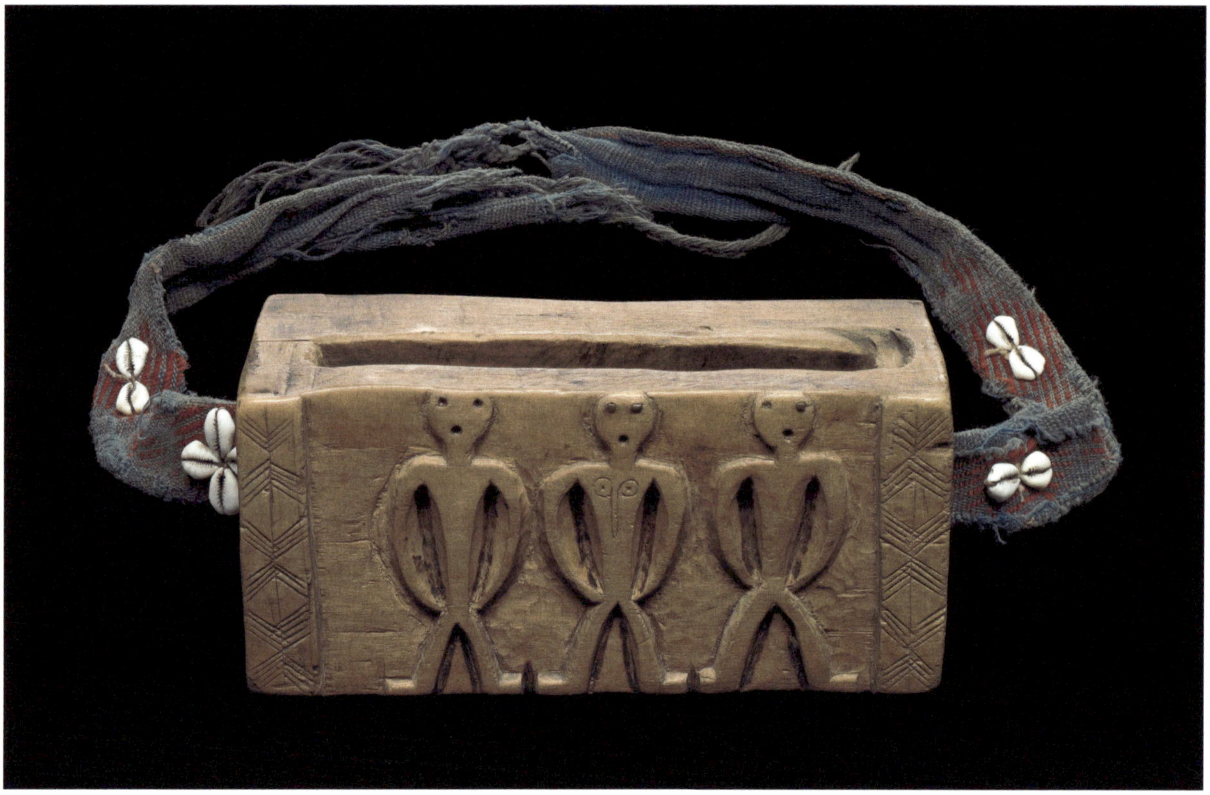

and the National Socialist Council of Nagalim (NSCN-IM), the most important resistance group, which was led by Isak Swu and Thuingaleng Muivah, the situation has improved.[7] Other rebel factions have, however, continued to fight, and there is still no prospect of a comprehensive political solution. As recently as December 2021 thirteen Naga who had been 'mistaken' for rebels were shot by the Assam Rifles, Indian special units. There were more Naga casualties in the unrest that followed. ——

The exhibition at the Humboldt Forum is based on the nineteenth-century Naga collection at the Berlin Ethnological Museum and contemporary objects acquired in Nagaland in 2019. Most of the objects on display are textiles. Changes in the techniques and materials used for clothing and its function are easy to read from these artefacts. Traditional customs and adaptation to changes in the way of living overlap. The exhibition also addresses the role of Christianity, the earlier significance of headhunting, the tattoo revival, fashion and social media. In addition, the use of vegetal materials and the links via those materials to a modern globalised world within Naga society are vividly shown in the 'Botany' section. Representing the society of origin, the artist Zubeni Lotha is showing works of her own. Zubeni Lotha cannot, of course, speak for the Naga in their entirety. More Naga voices can be heard on subjects such as Christianity, the significance of the exhibition for the Naga and headhunting in videos and audio stations at the exhibition. —— This book, too, is a collaborative project because most of the essays are the work of Naga writers reporting from the insider perspective. The primary objective is to involve people on site and also include their texts in this publication. Some of the writers are known worldwide. Dolly Kikon, for instance, writes about her role as a Naga anthropologist. Iris Odyuo, who has visited the Ethnologische Museum in Berlin in person, addresses the importance of European Naga collections to Naga living at home. Aküm Longchari, publisher of the

Fig. 2 Machete sheath (*nok leptsü*), Ao Naga, Nagaland, latter half 19th century, wood, cloth, cowrie shell

Samuel E. Peal Collection, donated in 1896 to the Royal Museum of Ethnology, Inv. No. IC28498, Staatliche Museen zu Berlin, Ethnologisches Museum

Fig. 3 Necklace for women (*wamkum*), Ao Naga, Molung Kimong, Nagaland, latter half 19th century, snail shells, carnelian stones, seeds

Adolf Bastian Collection, sold in 1879 to the Royal Museum of Ethnology, Inv. No. IC8476, Staatliche Museen zu Berlin, Ethnologisches Museum

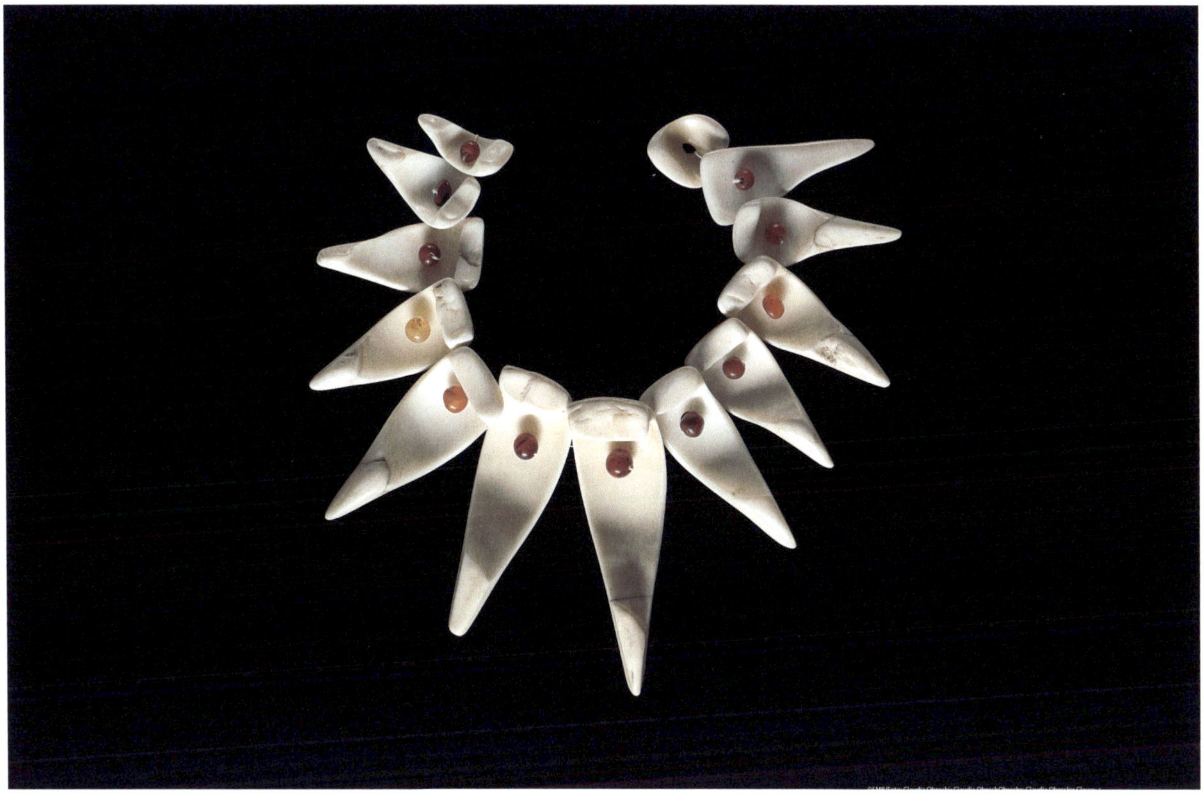

Morung Express, a Nagaland daily, analyses the traces of colonialism that are still palpably present today. The Naga writer Theyiesinuo Keditsu devotes herself to the subject of fashion and social media from the standpoint of identity issues whereas Elisabeth Seyerl-Langkamp goes into the meaning of Naga textiles from the colonial era to the present. Kathrin Grotz sheds light on the history of the collection from the aspect of botanical research in Nagaland. Roland Platz writes about the history of the collection and its provenance as well as its significance from the Western ethnological viewpoint. Zubeni Lotha, co-curator from Nagaland, describes her personal development as an artist and photographer and her connection with the political history of the Naga from the colonial past to the present.

1 Oppitz 2008, p. 12; Wouters 2017.

2 Stockhausen, in Oppitz 2008, p. 58.

3 Jacobs 2012, pp. 135–150.

4 Slash-and-burn agriculture, which leaves the root systems and stumps of trees in the soil. Vegetation is simply burnt away, with the ash serving as a natural fertiliser.

5 Drouyer 2016, p. 13.

6 Ibid., p. 23.

7 Phanjoubam 2016, p. 197.

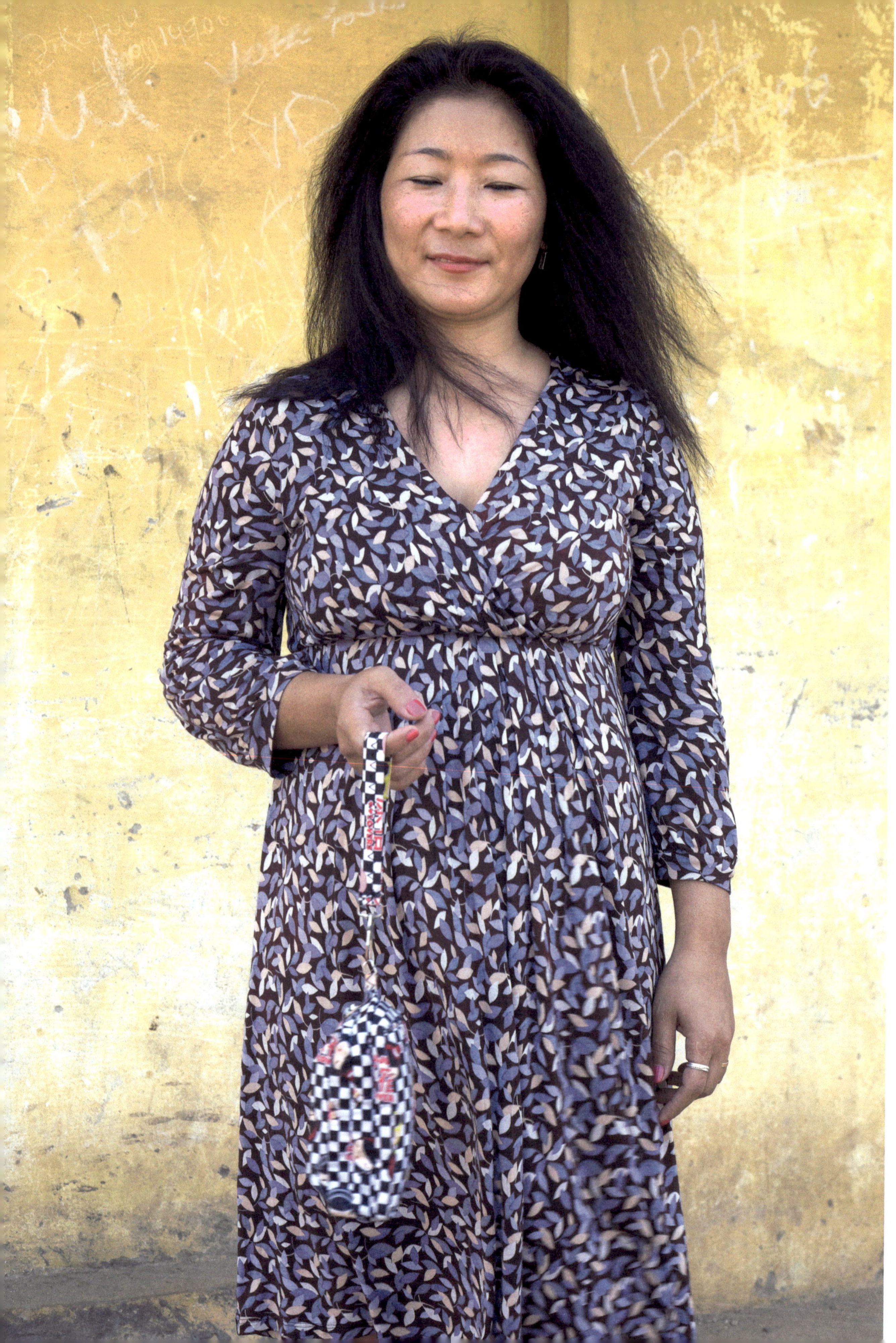

13

UNSEEING THE PAST

Zubeni Lotha

How do we memorialise our past in photographs? What does it mean to talk about the past in photography when every moment captured becomes the immediate past and we move on to the next photograph or image thus memorialising the past in an instant? Can the past be so immediate? Are the photographs truly a representation of our memories? When we talk of memories we talk of the authenticity of memories, but sometimes memories can also be about forgetting. They are not always about remembering. So, when we look at a photograph, what are we choosing to remember and to forget?

What am I choosing to represent when I take a photograph? Am I consciously memorialising the past? What about the anthropological photographs of the Nagas? When I look at them today, what am I remembering of the past? Do the photographs accurately represent the past for me or are they just photographs without any emotional or historical meaning? This leads me to question whether photographs are historical or emotional or both.

When I started to photograph my hometown of Dimapur from my memories, I slowly became more aware of the place in a way that I never was before. Of course, places had changed over the years, but that wasn't what surprised me; it was my associations that surprised me. I always saw the town through rose-tinted lenses. Despite most of my childhood being spent indoors under strict instructions not to venture out by myself, I never questioned the restrictions and Dimapur was a safe bubble for me. I never questioned the palpable fear around me as I was growing up, from growing tensions between the Indian armies and the Naga freedom fighters.

Fig. 1–3 Zubeni Lotha, No title

My parents tried to shield us from the ever-present violence by sending us to boarding schools in another city. The freedom struggle of the Nagas for a sovereign nation apart from India was always in the background of our conversations, as well as the restrictive actions of my parents because the times were tumultuous and violence was never far off. But my holidays away from my boarding school were a time to be home with family and friends, and to read and watch television and be lazy – so oblivious to the world collapsing around so many people. The town, I realised as I started to photograph, was a blur to me. Most of my memories were unravelling, bringing to my mind other memories, which I had chosen to ignore, to not speak of or think of, in the process forgetting some of my past. Memories also can show our prejudices and biases, our own misconceptions, and the way we view the world around us. Photographing Dimapur also allowed me talk about the history of the city and engage with it in a way I had not attempted before, when I just wanted to escape from it. There were a lot of hidden memories which I realised many people were scared or ashamed to talk about, but they needed to be shared. There were so many broken dreams and shattered hopes, and I realised this town was like any other place with all of its hopes and fears and joys mingled together, weaving a fabric of different lives, creating unique histories and stories. My photographs were becoming a past the moment my fingers pressed the shutter down with a finality.

Looking at the anthropological photographs of the Nagas from the colonial era, I always catch myself trying to imagine their lives. The images should be talking to me about my ancestors' lives, their stories, but it is difficult for me to connect with these photographs. They show warrior-like men finely attired in elaborate headgear, and sometimes they have tattoos on their bodies or faces, sometimes they show them with their javelin held high, as if to fling it in the air at some unseen enemy. The women decked in beautiful jewellery or partially undressed, exposing some of their body, unconscious of their

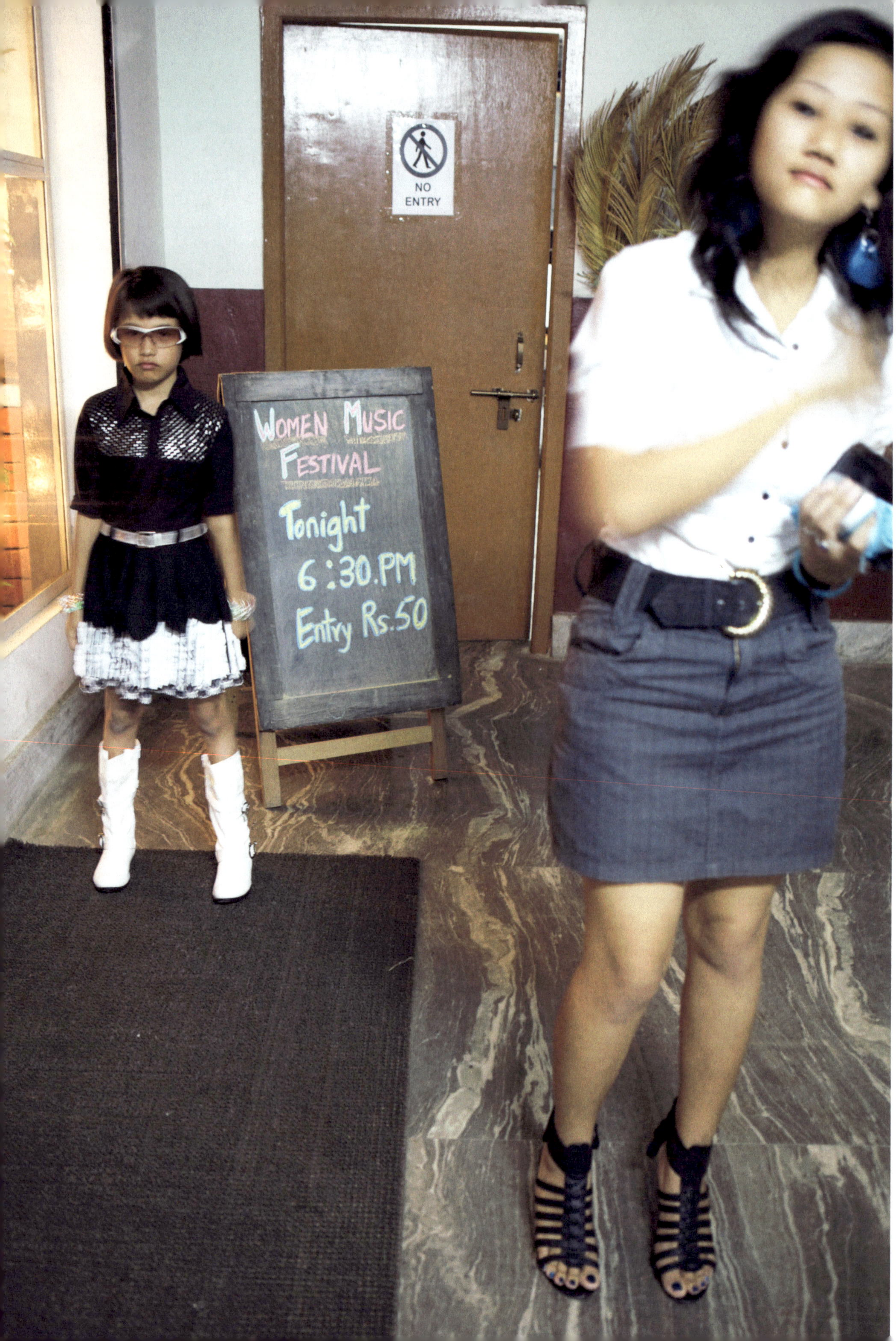
NO
ENTRY
WOMEN MUSIC
FESTIVAL
Tonight
6:30.PM
Entry Rs.50

15

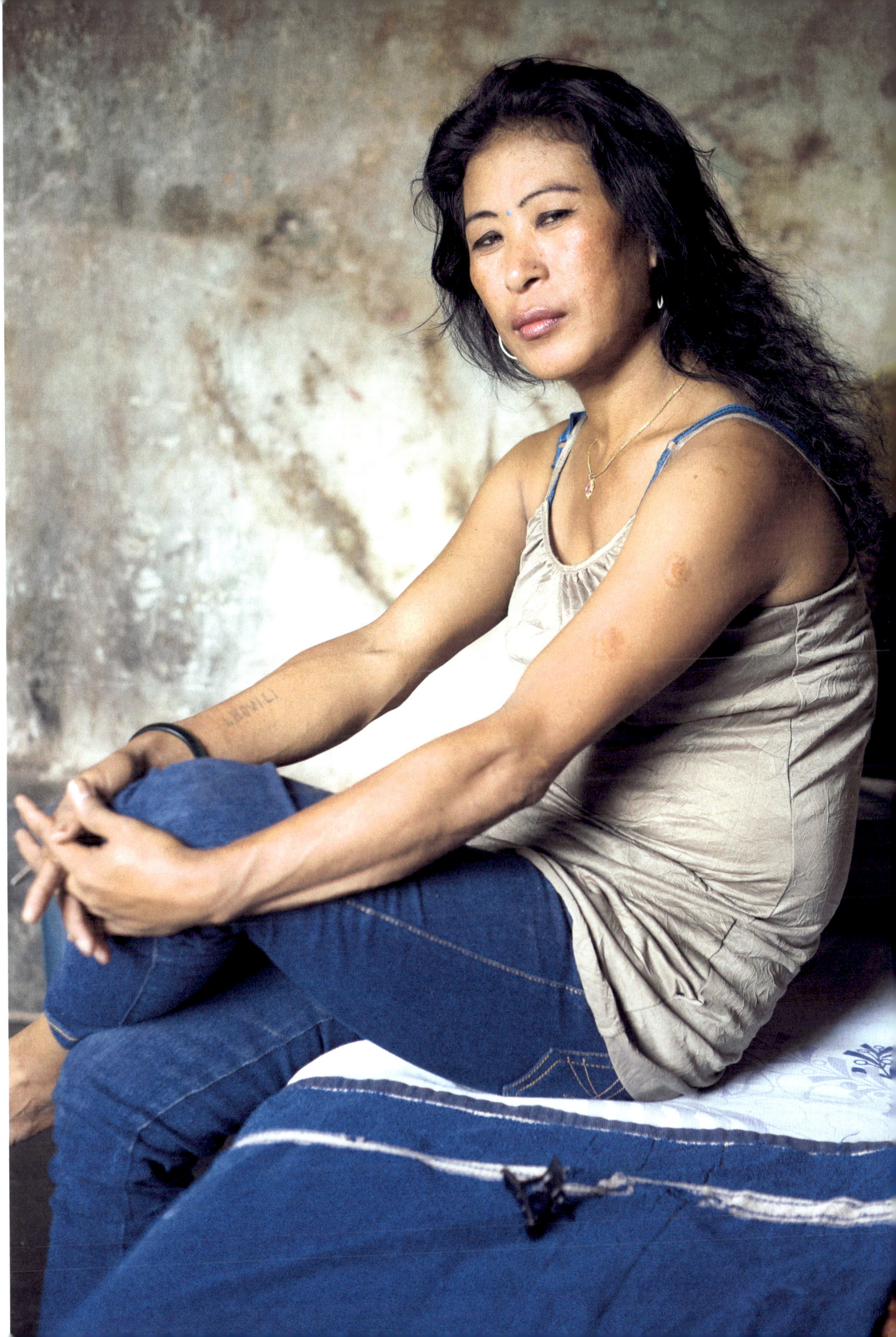

bareness. Many photographs showing men and women richly dressed in traditional costume in the act of dancing. All the photographs I sense are meant to evoke a sense of nostalgia for a way of life fast disappearing. Sometimes the frames are too narrow and I cannot see beyond the photographs. I don't know what I am supposed to be imagining when I look at such beautiful, exotic photographs, which are meant to be a big part of my history. I can always sense the power positions when I look at such photographs: the privileged 'white' colonial person with his new modern technology peeping into a very simple tribal world far away from all modern progress and technology. It is the technology of the camera and the bearer of that technology that speaks volumes when I look at the colonial/anthropological photographs. Sometimes it makes for uncomfortable viewing, such blatant projection of the roles of power. And the more I look into the historical photographs of the Nagas, the more aware I become of something that as a photographer myself I start to realise, and that is that photographs are not really true representatives of the people photographed or their lives – they are more the photographer's vision of the world which he or she is seeing.

It is not what is seen in the photographs that captures my attention, but what is left out of the photographs that I start to think about. But then memories are also sometimes not about what we remember, but what we have chosen to forget or what we naturally forget. And maybe we need certain associations to bring back those memories sometimes – maybe that is what my photographs about my hometown did for me.

For the purposes of the questions I posed in the beginning, I have chosen to talk about some of the photographs from my Dimapur project which I started as a way of re-visiting my memories of the town. What sort of memories did such associations bring out in my mind? I also look at some of the historical photographs of the Naga people to explore my questions.

This photograph |fig. 4| was taken at a building site. The moment I saw the image something about it struck me, and I knew I had to photograph it. It is just a wall with cement running down the points. This photograph reminded me of the stories I heard from people I met while photographing Dimapur. Two stories in particular stand out. One is about my friend whom I met after many years. She narrated an event in her life about the loss of her brother, which was brutal and horrific. She told me they found his body shot and tossed in the jungle, but even today she has no conclusion to the story because she does not know who shot him or for what reason. The other story is about a person I was introduced to. I saw her in front of the grave of her brother. He was also shot dead when he was just sixteen years old, and he lays buried in the garden of her home – forever a cruel reminder of a life snatched away so young. The 1980s and the 1990s, the time of the exploration of my memories, were very tumultuous decades for the Nagas. Violence did not only mean gun violence or the fierce encounters between the Indian armies and the Naga fighters, it also meant the peak time of drug and alcohol abuse. Through the stories of drug and alcohol abuse one can understand the emotional cruelty that families went through for years. How can such pain and violence be photographed? These are just two stories among the many painful stories of loss. This photograph for me captures the tears of such pain and loss.

Another example of loss and grief is this photograph of graffiti on a wall located in an area which experienced a lot of violence and death during the 1990s |fig. 5|. The graffiti is of a Lotha Naga name, Mhathung, and *Nzan* means 'love'. It could be an ode to a person gone or a loved one remembered – such a fleeting tribute, because that wall no longer exists today.

One photograph is simply a painting I happened to see on a busy roadside |fig. 6|. It was in a small stand off a busy road where a painter was selling his paintings, almost obscured by moving vehicles and pedestrians going about their busy lives. I saw the painting while stuck in a traffic jam. I parked the car and

Fig. 4–6 Zubeni Lotha, No title

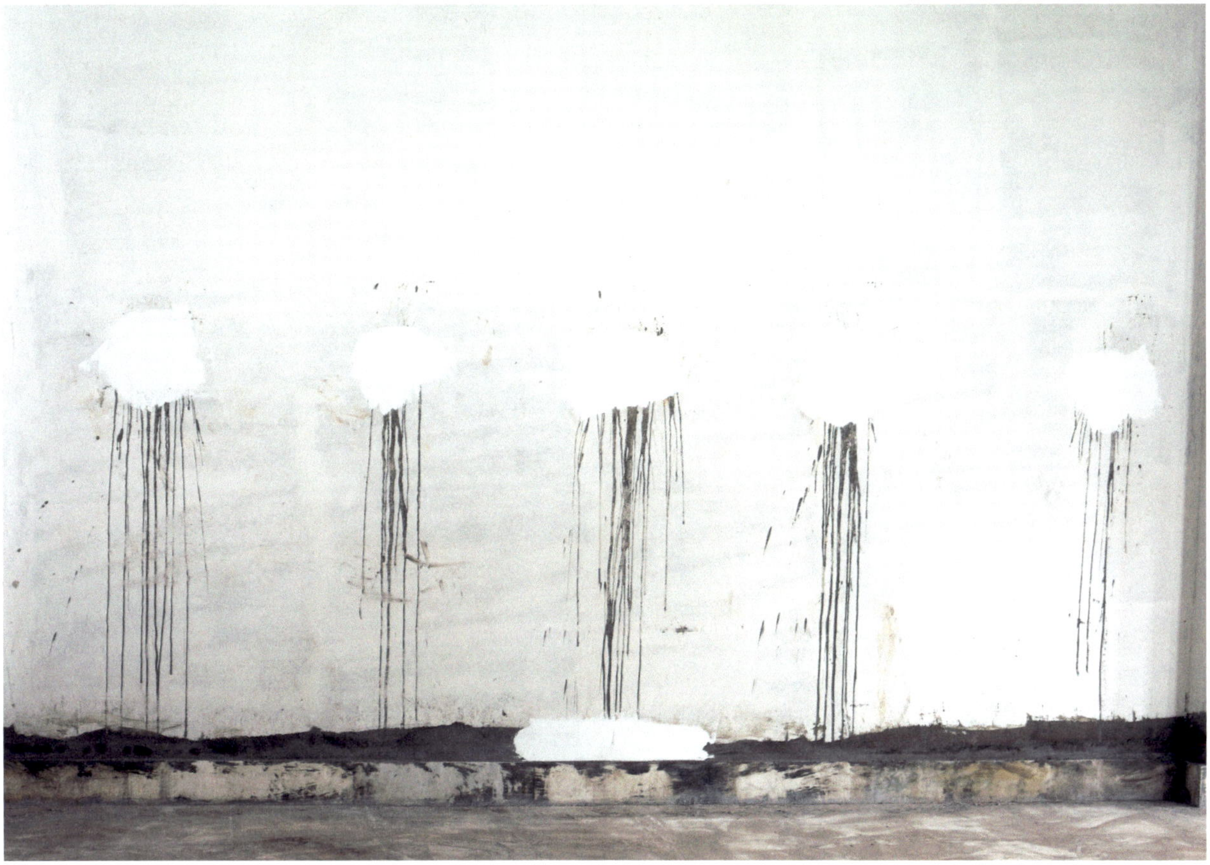

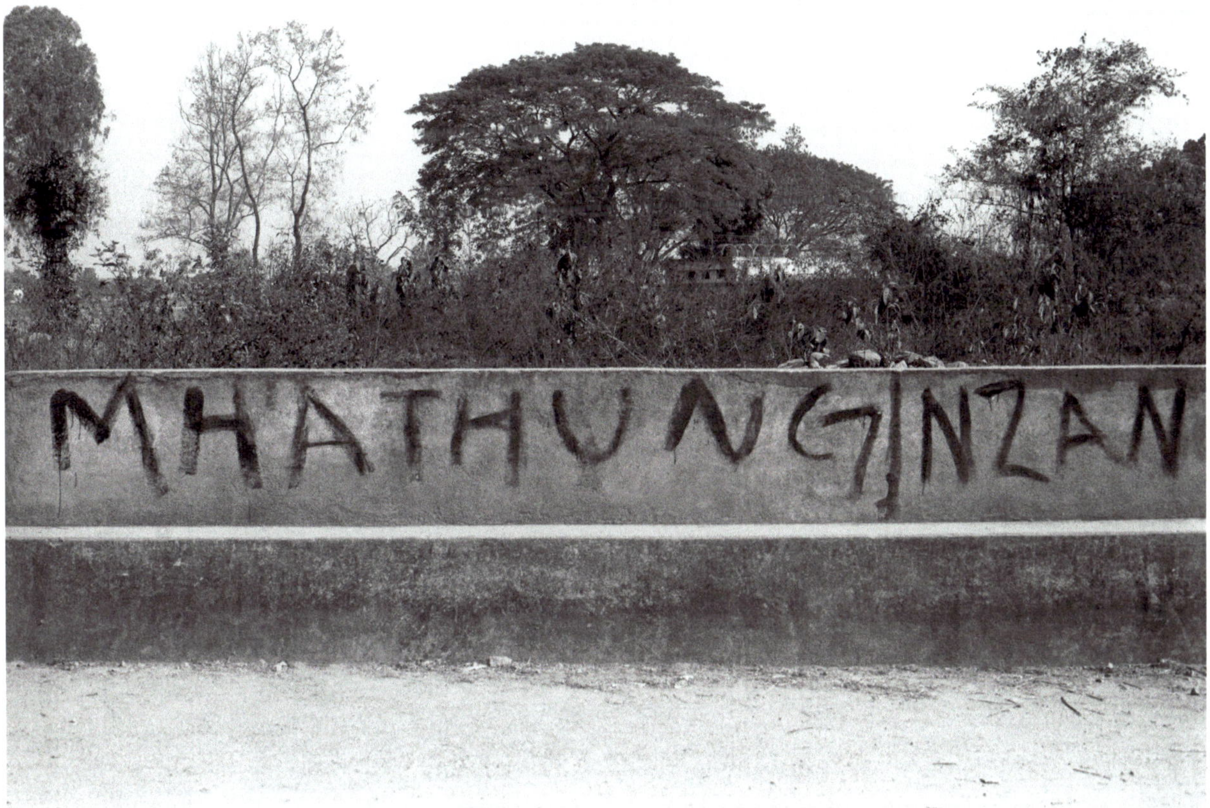
MHATHUNG NZAN

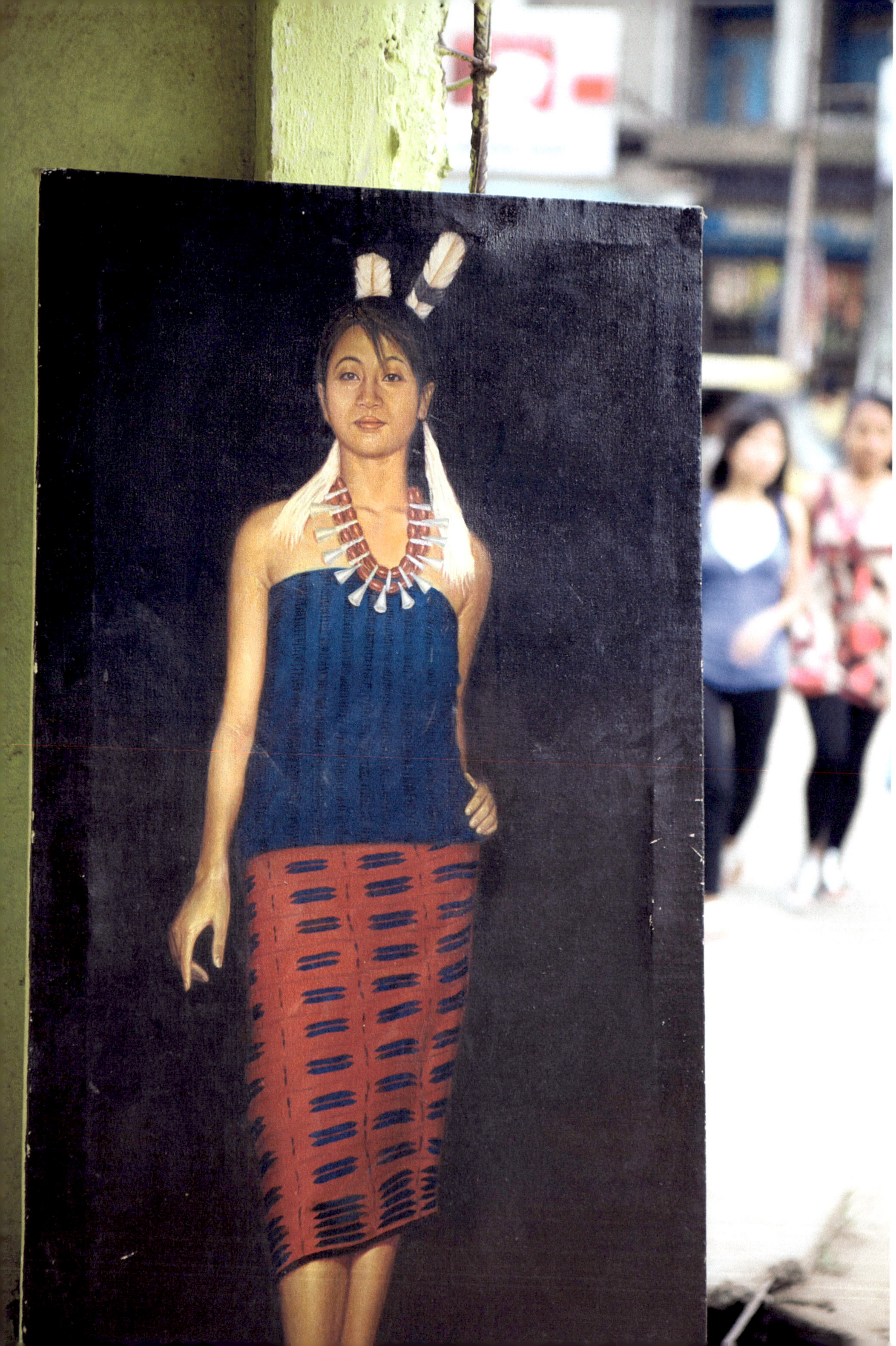

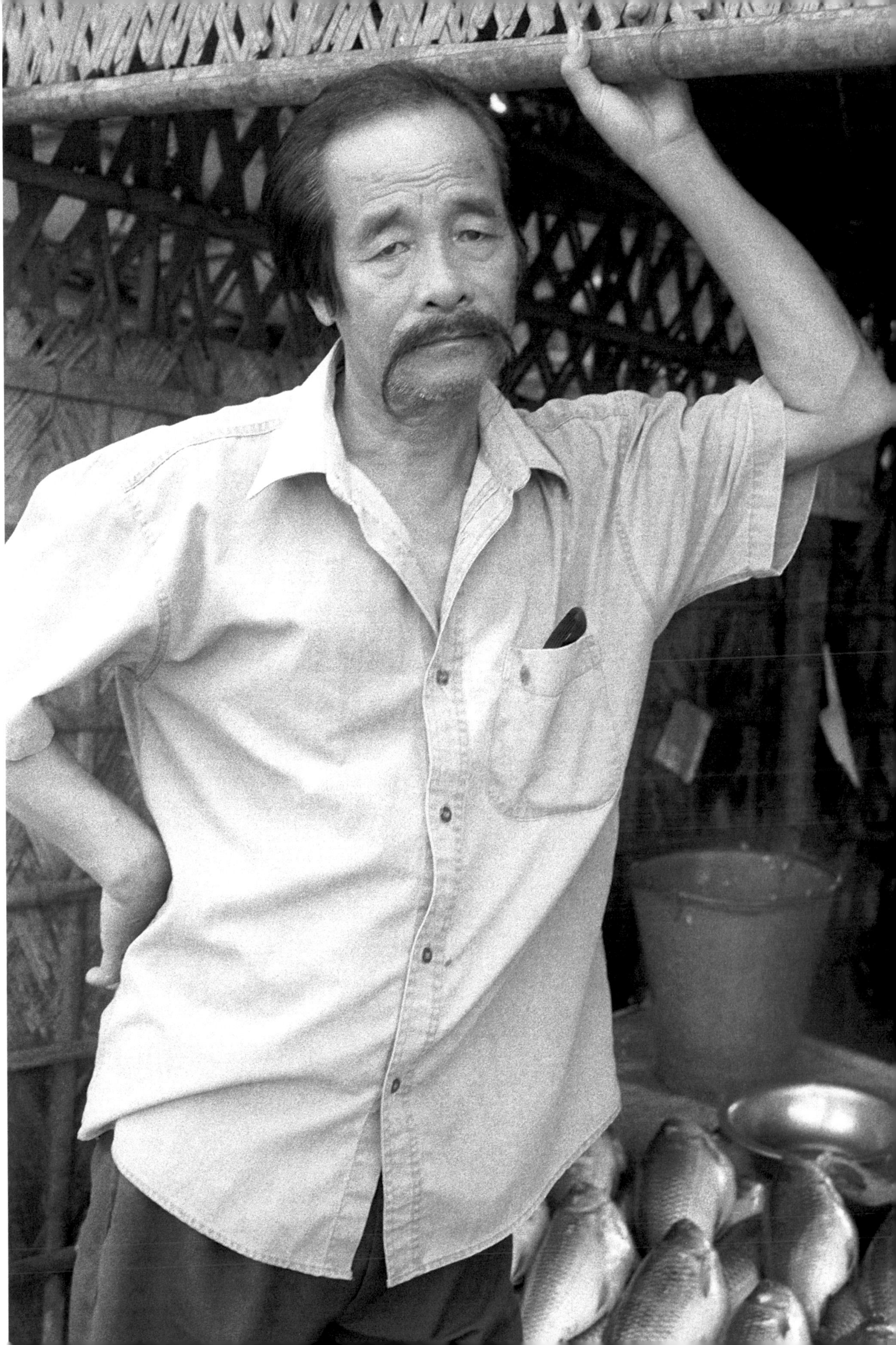

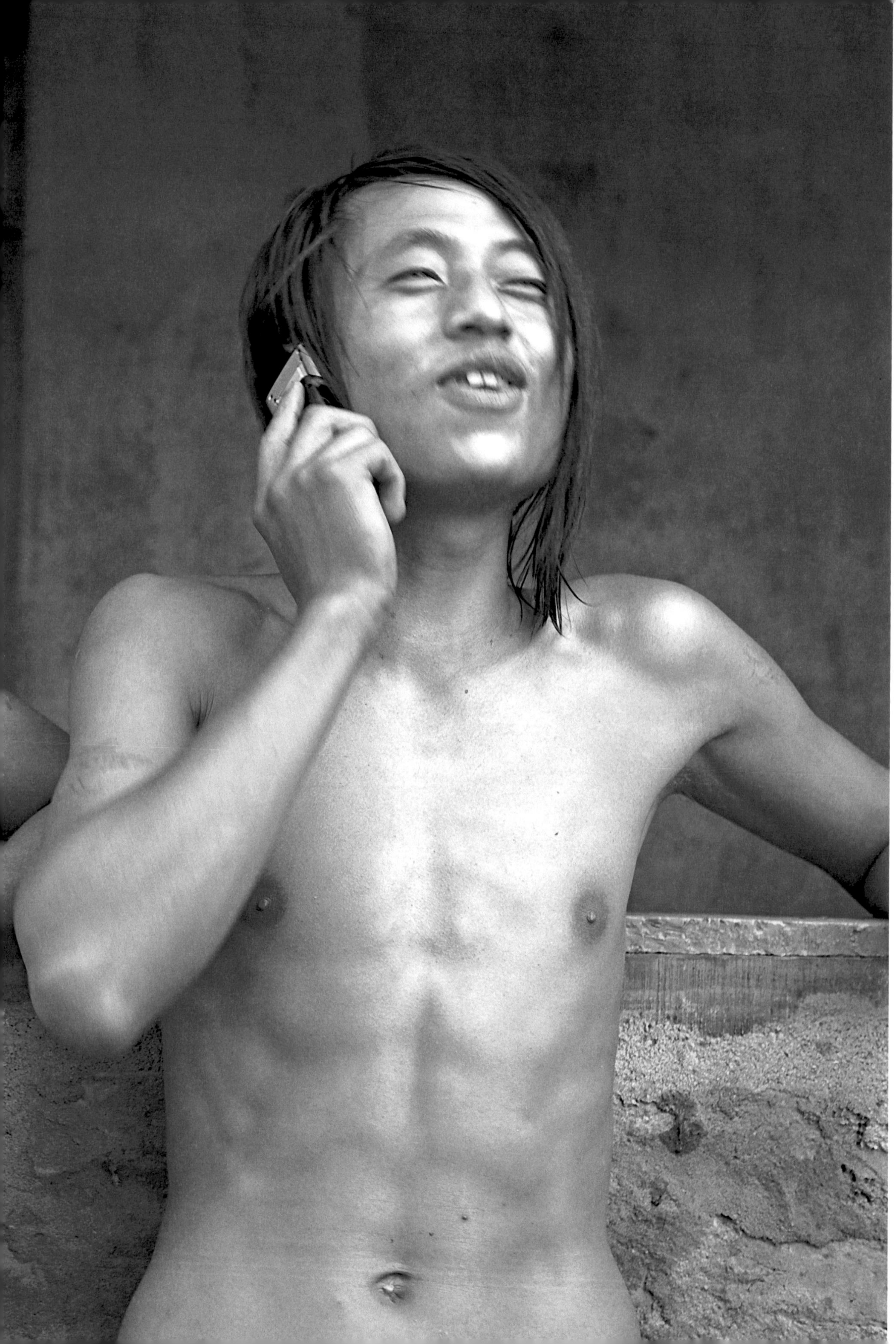

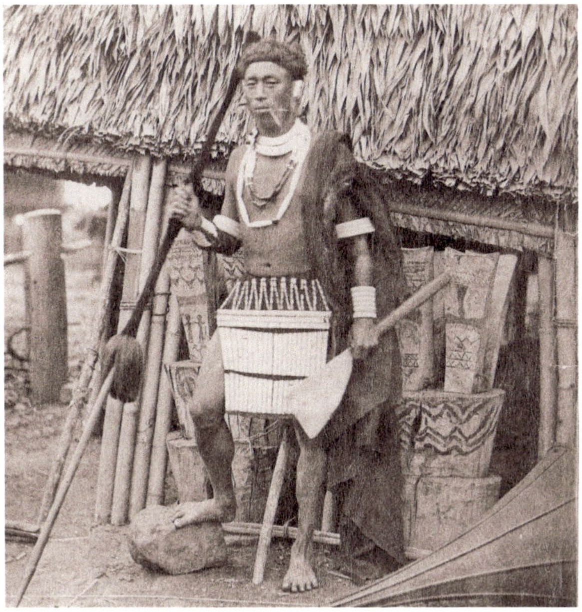

quickly got out to take the photo because I thought how exotic the girl looked in her traditional attire, and in that instant I was the outsider with a camera looking at an exotic tribal girl and I had to photograph her – which in a way points out my own stereotyping. So, I waited for a few seconds till I saw two girls walking towards me and then I pressed the shutter. But by making the painting dominate the frame, I wanted to drive home the point that even as a photographer I would automatically always look for the exotic or the different to tell a story. But is this a real story? ———

It was also important to capture the essence or feel of the town. And some of the people I met on the street while photographing caught my imagination |fig. 7–8|. Dimapur is a small town that just keeps expanding. It is hot and humid for most of the year. While it is a booming commercial town now, it still retains a certain laidback attitude, maybe because of the intense summer heat, or maybe a carryover from its small-town days. The town itself is not pretty and tourists can easily give it a miss as they drive on towards the hill areas for the cooler climate and prettier landscape. But in the midst of all the commerce and the chaos of everyday living, there is a certain unique charm to the town. ———

In my historical photographs, I chose to look at the photographs that the Ethnological Museum in Berlin has in their collection |fig. 9–12|.

The photographs already become a past even before they are shot, because the intention of these photographs is for the purposes of documenting the material culture that is being acquired as a collection. These photographs are being 'museumified'. The photographs show beautifully composed pictures of people in rich, exotic costumes in a remote land, where people live in thick forests. There is no interaction or engagement with the people or the place. The power of the camera is very visible. Most of the frames are tightly composed, and the people within the frames are flattened against the background, which is used as a prop to accentuate the people in the foreground – maybe that background prop is their house, their field, their village or a structure they built. As a viewer, I have no borders or edges to look into, no place for my mind to wander, but to look at the photograph presented to me. Most photographs are two-dimensional and flat. I have to be a bit more forgiving with these photographs because their purpose is different; they are not trying to capture the Naga people's reality. But even the anthropological photographs are not dissimilar, although the purpose is to study the lives of the people and their world. It would be unfair for me to judge the historical image

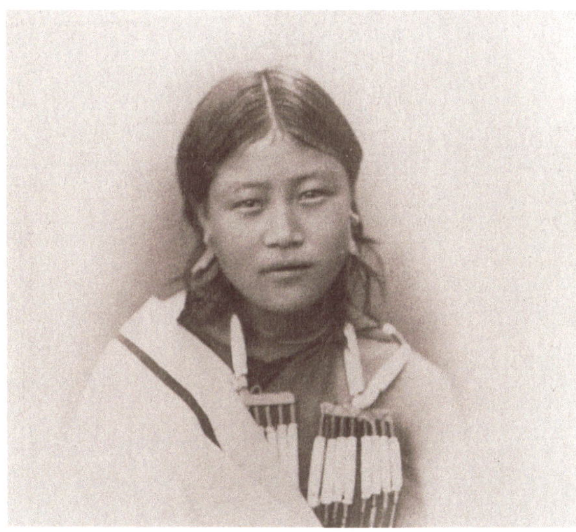

Fig. 7–8 Zubeni Lotha, No title

Fig. 9 Ao Naga warrior
Otto E. Ehlers, c. 1890
Staatliche Museen zu Berlin, Ethnologisches Museum, Inv. No. VIII C 4622b

Fig. 10 Angami Naga girl
Otto E. Ehlers, c. 1890
Staatliche Museen zu Berlin, Ethnologisches Museum Berlin, Inv. No. VIII C 4621c

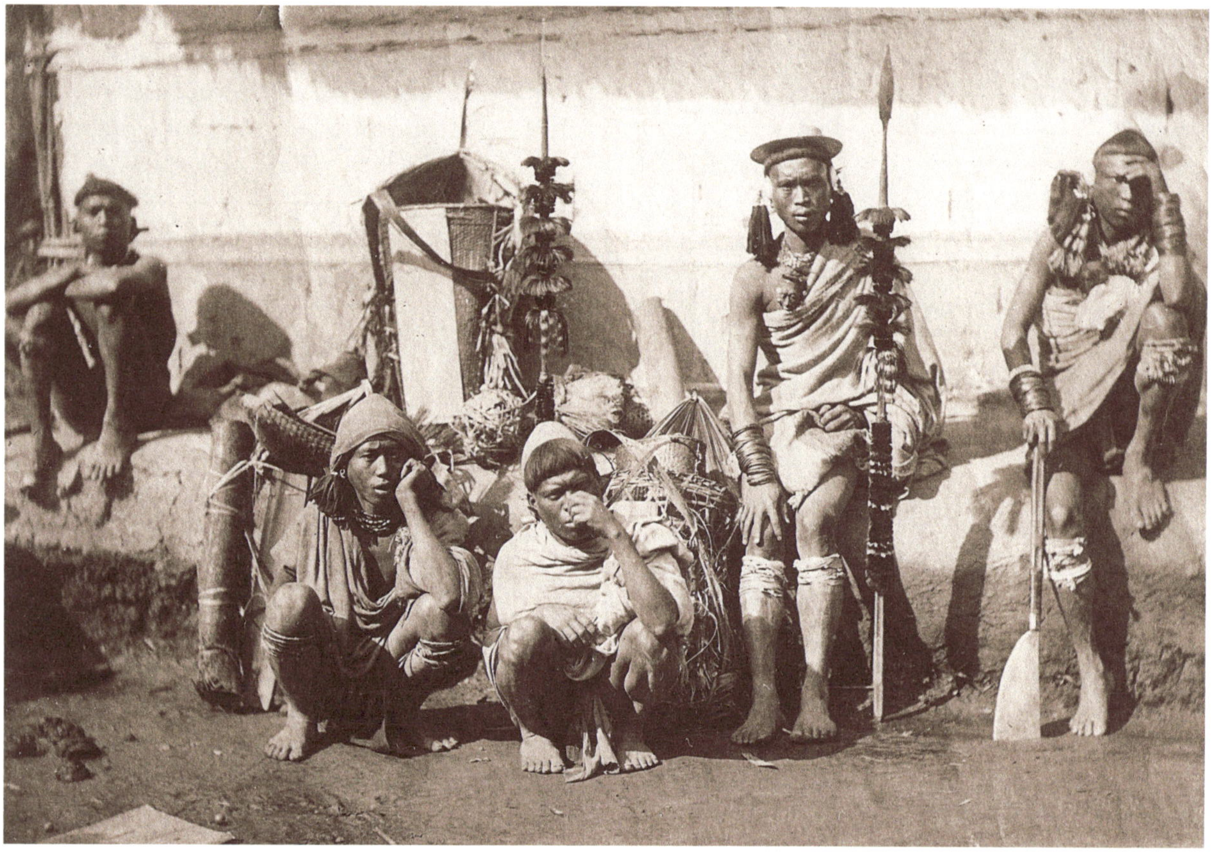

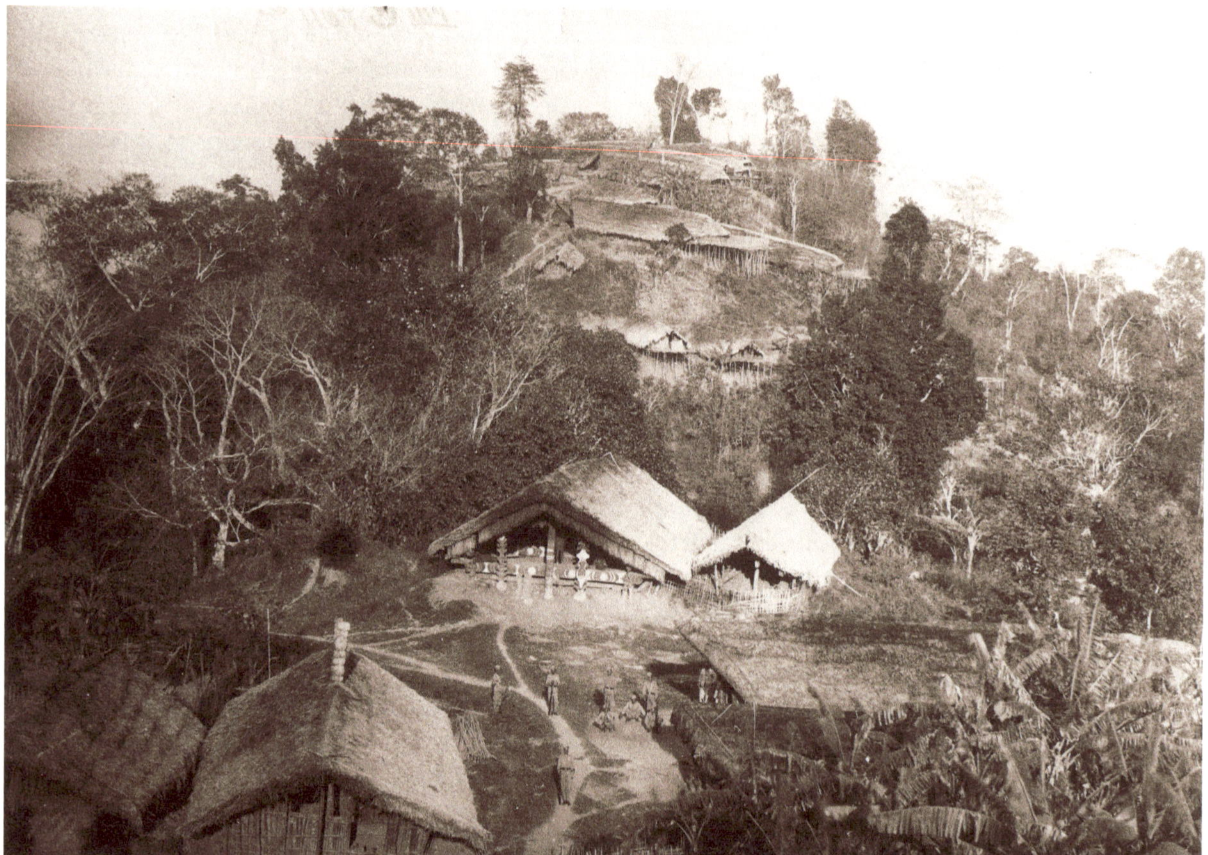

as the work of a photographer, but these are the only historical photographs of the Nagas available. And these photographs have influenced the readings or 'stereotyping' of the Nagas for decades. In these photographs the past becomes so much a focus or even a part of the present. In the popular cultural Hornbill Festival in Nagaland, these 'historical' photographs are often recreated as if to show the 'authentic' culture/tradition of the Nagas – a past that for the most part was written and photographed by the colonialists and their partners. The photographs show no participation of the subjects and no interaction with the camera. But for me, I am thankful that such historical photographs exist, whether they show certain biases or whether they are viewed through a certain perspective, because these colonial photographs are the only historical photographs of the Nagas available and it helps me in understanding how to look at the past and the present, and helps me to critique my own work, my culture, my past or even my memories. They also show how the 'Western eye' continues to influence the way Nagas are viewed from the outside, and even from within. And they help to show how the Nagas in turn perpetuate these images to a certain degree in trying to explain themselves or their culture to the world. ——

I don't think my questions have found final answers, but photography for me is a way of continuously exploring these questions, and maybe the answer will not be found because we are continuously creating our many different pasts. There are many ways of talking about the pasts with many differing opinions. This is just one of them.

Fig. 11 Group of Naga warriors

Otto E. Ehlers, c. 1890
Staatliche Museen zu Berlin, Ethnologisches Museum, Inv. No. VIII C 4631c

Fig. 12 A Nangta Naga village

Otto E. Ehlers, c. 1890
Staatliche Museen zu Berlin, Ethnologisches Museum, Inv. No. VIII C 4611c

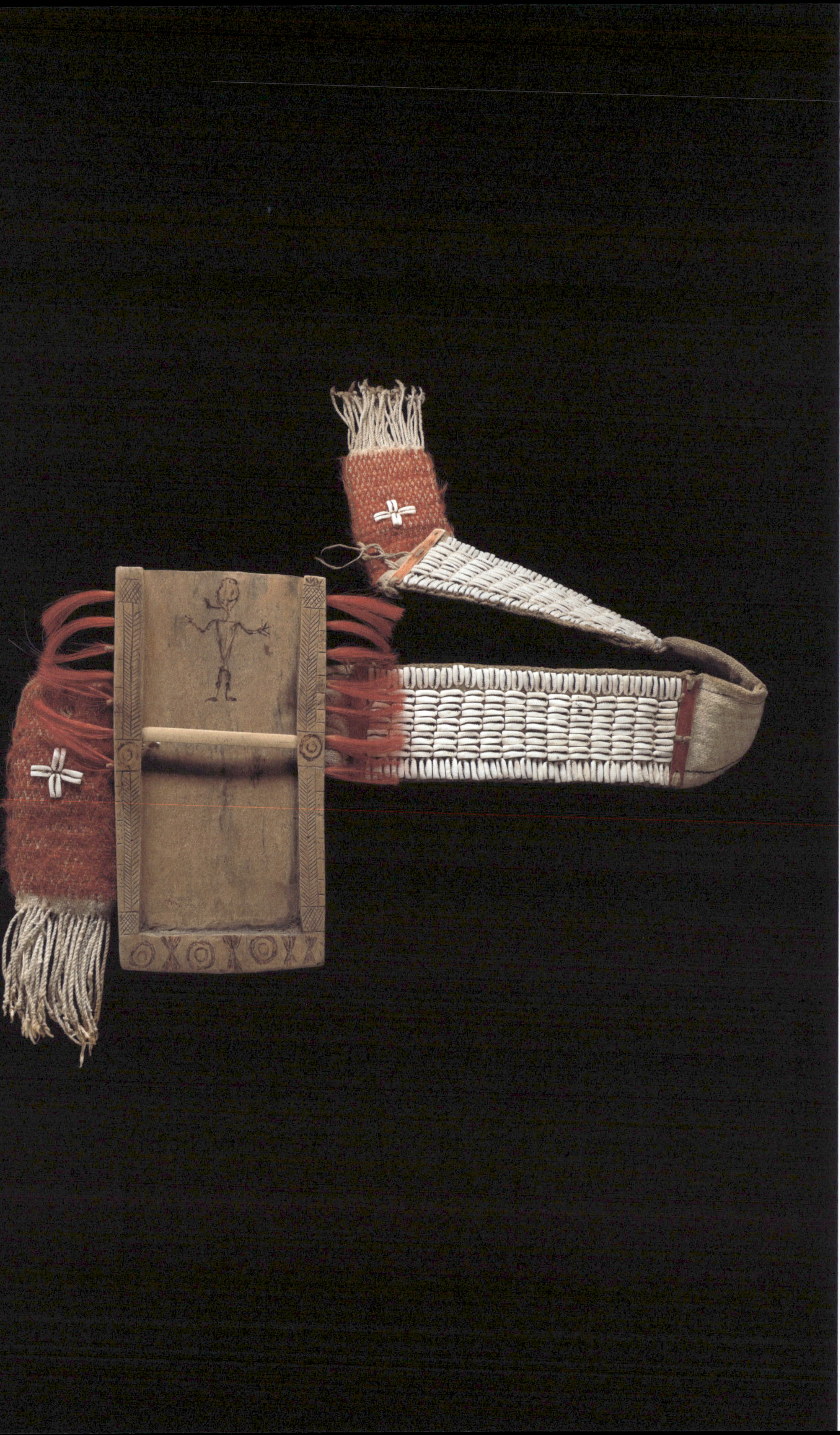

'A CAPTURED NATION'[1]

Aküm Longchari

The intrusion of British colonial forces into Naga territories marked a rude interruption of a people's way of living, their independence, their worldview and their self-rule. The British discovered the 'strategic value of the mountains' and in varying degrees engaged in 'punitive expeditions'[2] and 'economic break-up and incorporation of the Naga hills into their market sphere, combined with the threat of military force'.[3] Marcus Franke informs us that 'the trade goods and opportunities were meant to be the carrot; the striking power of the *sepoys*,[4] the stick'.[5] The intent of pursuing this de facto policy was to subjugate the Nagas. Like most colonial powers, the British constructed a language consistent with the purposes of colonial anthropology that was designed to legitimise colonial rule.

The colonial encroachment dehumanised the Nagas and breached their self-determining capacity and ability as makers of their own destiny. Ali Mazrui's illustration of the caravan of culture[6] captures a vivid image of the colonial experience. To contextualise Mazrui's illustration: the Naga people are meandering towards their own destination under the stars of history. In the course of their journey, a major interruption takes place, and the Naga caravan is overcome and hijacked by outsiders. The intruders diverted the Naga caravan away from its natural route, taking it into an alluring, but strange destination.

Throughout this time, the Naga people try to free the caravan and guide it by Naga values and aspirations following their own direction and destiny. However, the caravan continues to be diverted a considerable distance from its original route. Now, the Nagas stand at an intersection: Do they continue down the path of diversion, relocate to the point of diversion and find their natural route, or chart a new path of their choosing? This dilemma is faced not just by the Nagas, but generally by colonised and Indigenous peoples around the world. —

According to Roy Burman, the 'Naga Conflict appears to have surfaced after the British East India Company started flexing its politico-territorial control after defeating the Burmese and signing of the Yandabo Treaty in 1826.'[7] Since then, the colonial infringement marked the beginning of a long-fragmented history of resistance, dissent, torment, resilience, militarisation, oppression, domination, trauma and destruction. Yet, the experience bore stories of courage, forgiveness, healing, the dream to become fully human, the ability to appreciate the gifts of life, laughter and the eagerness to live freely in peaceful coexistence.

Above all, it stirred a national consciousness for freedom and re-humanisation that continues to this day. Nandita Haksar, a lawyer in the Supreme Court of India, says anyone wanting to understand the Naga spirit should 'read Asterix and Obelix, about the little Gaul village which defied the Roman Empire'.[8]

The Naga territory is a homeland of permanently established village republics which are perched on mountain-tops, looking down into the valleys. For Andrew Gray, these Naga democratic 'village states' were 'likened to Greek city states, an image which Britain used at that time to conjure up as the height of civilization' with 'cultured nobility'.[9] This, he suggests, was one of the reasons why Nagas were 'excluded ... from the hierarchical influences of the plains'.[10] Simultaneously, the 'fascination with savagery' and the emphasis on head-hunting and nakedness created images of the 'wild tribal people'.[11]

Gray says the imagery can be described in two concepts – 'savage and noble' – and adds that the British both 'admired and feared' the Nagas.[12] Ironically, both these characterisations, he points out, were used against the Naga recognition of independence and self-determination. The Nagas were 'isolated and

Fig. 1 *Dao* (machete) sheath, Nyishi (hist. Miri Naga), Arunachal Pradesh, latter half 19th century, bone, hair, wood, cowrie shells

Otto E. Ehlers Collection, donated in 1896 to the Royal Museum of Ethnology, Inv. No. IC28552, Staatliche Museen zu Berlin, Ethnologisches Museum

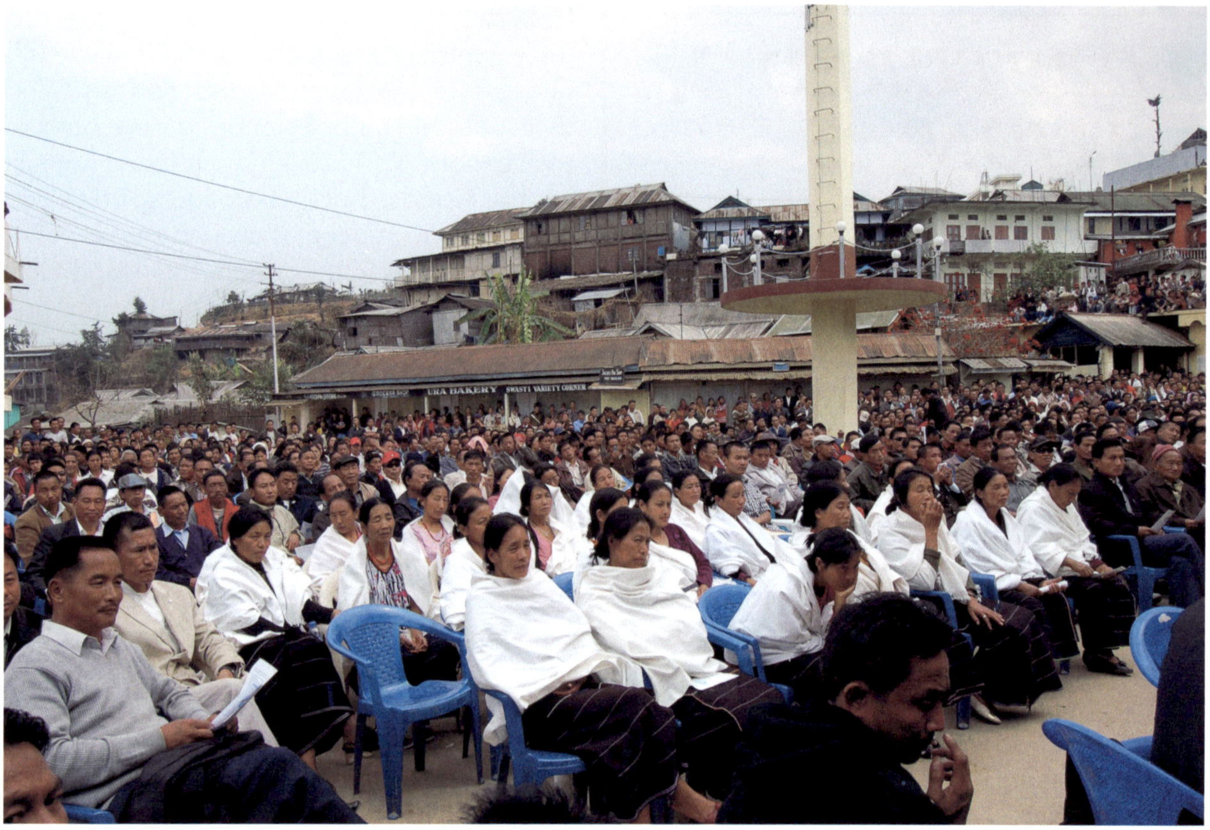

underdeveloped', effectively caught between two British territories: British India and British Burma.[13] Colin Johnson informs us that British incursion into Naga territories was followed by missionary activity and observes that, 'today though most Nagas have long been Christian, many are still ambiguous about the missionary activity and the benefits and harm it has done'.[14]

Nicholas B. Dirks emphasises that colonisation was 'not just the result of the power of superior arms, military organisation, political power, or economic wealth', but was 'made possible, then sustained and strengthened, as much by cultural technologies of rule'.[15] Colonisation was part of a broader colonial project in which the production of colonial knowledge was essential. Dirks highlights that, 'colonial conquest was about the production of an archive of (and for) rule.'[16] Until today, the Nagas' pre-colonial history remains relatively unknown, and Naga history post-1826 is based on the products of colonial anthropology and colonial knowledge.

J. H. Hutton and J. P. Mills, two anthropologists and administrators in the Indian Civil Service during the British colonial rule,[17] were largely responsible for 'anthropological rule' over the Nagas.[18] Hence, the Naga way of living was reduced and caged within their 'anthropological framework of administration'.[19] Colonialism, Gray affirms, 'is not just a matter of one country taking over another. It is a series of economic and political relations which work against the right of self-determination.'[20] The interplay of colonial knowledge and colonial rule were the defining elements of colonisation. For the British, 'war was not the continuation of politics with other means, the policy was war'.[21]

The experience under colonial rule aroused Naga consciousness to become aware that they were culturally and politically unique, and their desire to retain their uniqueness was demonstrated by their resistance.[22] As Marcus Franke infers, 'This consciousness of being different qual-

Fig. 2 Phek, 28 February 2010. Naga women wearing traditional white shawls demonstrate their yearning for Nagas to be reconciled at the public meeting on Naga reconciliation. This meeting was part of the FNR's Journey of Common Hope when the FNR and the JWG (comprised of the Naga political groups that signed the Covenant of Naga Reconciliation) travelled to Naga towns and villages demonstrating their commitment to Naga reconciliation.

ifies to be called national, in the sense of a self-conscious political community'.[23] While Christianity was 'an aid in unifying the people',[24] the Naga exposure to the world through both World Wars was crucial in consolidating Naga nationalism.

In fact, while recalling the camaraderie developed by the 4,000 odd Nagas sent to Europe as part of the Allied forces during the First World War, Johnson asserts, 'It may be said that on the battlefields of France and in the trenches the iron spearhead of a new Naga nationalism was forged.'[25] By forming the Naga Club in 1918, the Nagas sought to create a new independent political identity. On 10 January 1929, the Naga Club made a submission to the British Statutory Commission stating that Nagas should be left alone 'to determine for ourselves as in ancient times'.[26]

For Franke, the 'Nagas realised that the British would not remain on the subcontinent forever and so had started their own national movement for the regaining of their sovereignty.'[27] Gray adds, 'It was the Naga people themselves who, understanding the nature of the colonial rule, mapped their independence which they had had before the British came onto a national identity which arose within the conditions of colonialism.'[28] However, Franke informs us that, the dramatic loss of standing and power in the course of the Second World War forced the British to retreat from the subcontinent and handover the Naga Hills to the successor creation, the Indian Union.[29]

Through this experience, it was evident that the British decision-makers never intended to give the Nagas their independence.[30] Johnson observes that the Naga decision for eventual independence may have been a reasonable solution. However, he points out that 'the option disappeared when the Labour Government came to power at the end of the Second World War and it was dropped as being unacceptable to both Indian and Burmese nationalist'.[31]

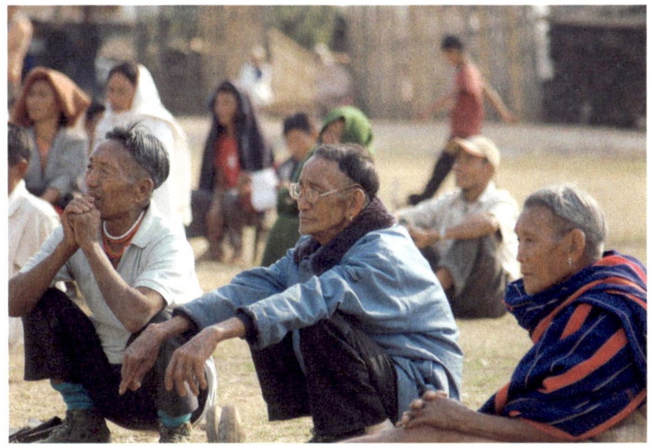

Fig. 3 Meluri, 27 February, 2010. Three Naga elders listen intently during a Naga reconciliation public meeting. The experience of witnessing the Naga Reconciliation process journeying through Naga towns and villages captured the Naga public's imagination. Since 2008, the Forum for Naga Reconciliation (FNR) has been engaged in a process of reconciliation and healing among the Naga Political Groups.
The Joint Working Group (JWG) was formed following three groups signing the 'Covenant of Naga Reconciliation' in 2009.
The FNR and JWG travelled to many Naga towns and villages to share and strengthen the Naga Reconciliation Process. Just witnessing the groups travel together to share their experiences captured the Naga public's imagination.

Nagas, along with other colonised people, sought to be free from colonial domination and regain their sovereignty. Through the Naga National Council (NNC), on 14 August 1947, they declared that 'Nagas will be independent' and 'must prevail regardless of size'.[32] To reaffirm this assertion, the NNC launched a Naga Voluntary Plebiscite on 16 May 1951, where a majority voted to be independent. Gray points out that Nagas, through these two political acts, 'affirmed their independence as the chosen manifestation of their self-determination'.[33]

Wati Aier, a Naga scholar and elder, reminds us that nationalism for the Naga people is 'a frame of mind which rises from the awareness of our memory and our self-hood'.[34] This, Aier adds, 'is our identity, and our common memory ... [and] is linked to self-determination. To be sure, the form of self-determination is nationalism.' A young Naga woman confirms that to be 'self-determining is not the end, but the means to an end'.[35]

Tragically, the decolonisation process was reduced to geopolitical adjustments,[36] and the political and geographical construct of the former colonisers has been maintained. The restricted application of self-determination contradicted the universality of self-determination as a right of all people. What exist today are borders that once served as administrative boundaries of colonial powers.[37] While imperialism ends where consent begins, the Nagas refused to give their consent to be

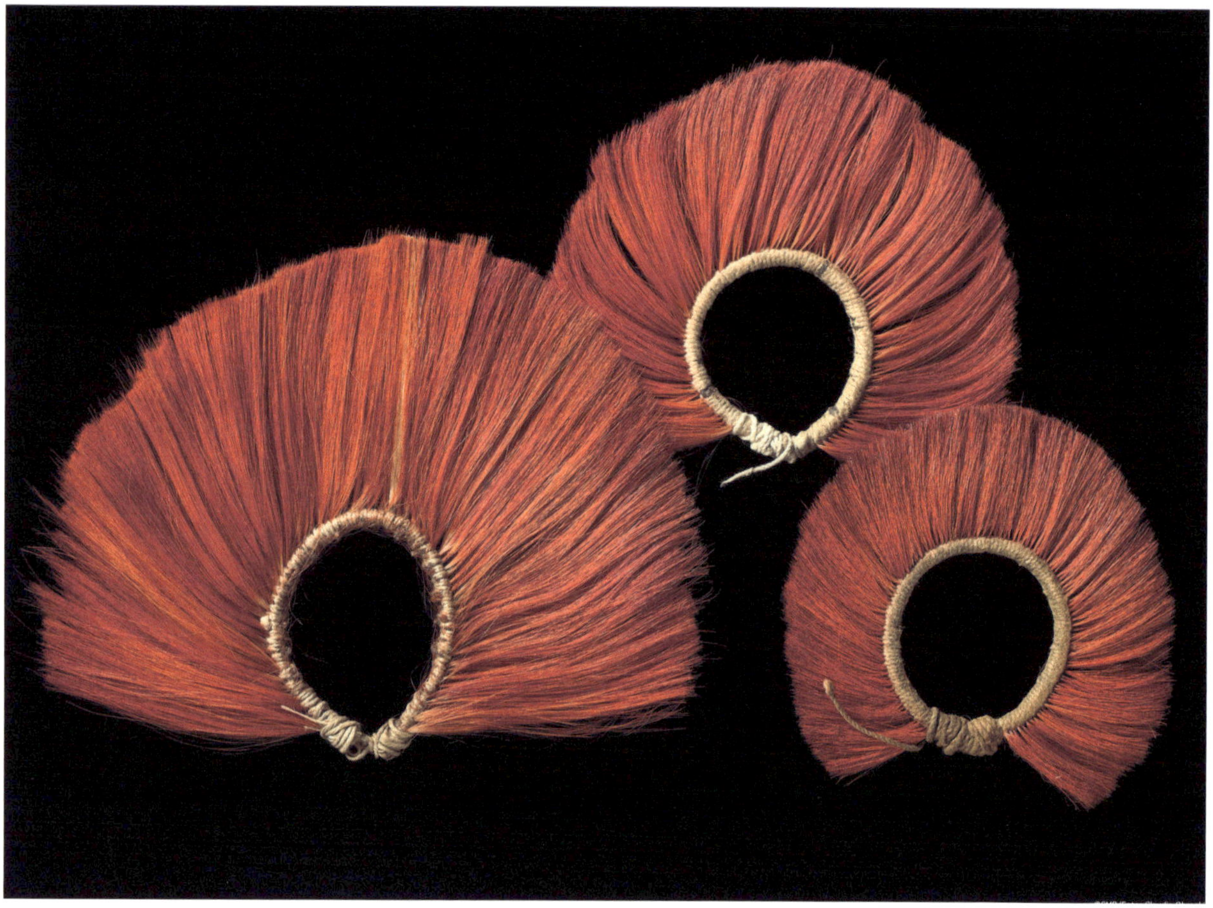

part of the Indian Union.[38] This in turn led to 'one of the world's least-known, but longest-running and bloodiest armed conflicts [and] one that has cost thousands of lives'.[39]

Naga leaders have made efforts to explore a peaceful transition, but since India was concerned that Naga territory would be isolated between India and China, they were determined to make it a part of India.[40] The Nagas wanted to recover their humanity and exercise their right of self-determination, but were reduced to a fragment, and found themselves either in India or Burma by the international boundary that arbitrarily divided their homeland. 'From this stage', Johnson observes, 'the whole tragedy of the Naga people has begun, and they are still seeking the end of the tragedy.'[41]

Nearly 195 years after the Naga conflict began with the incursion of the British colonial powers, the Nagas are in the midst of a ceasefire with the Indian State that began in 1997. 'The ceasefire in the Naga hills', Franke exclaims, 'is a product of the war that is the consequence of the continuation of conquest and subjugation.'[42]

Eventually, the Naga caravan seeks humanisation as affirmed by the yearning for freedom, justice and peace, by virtue of which Nagas can freely determine their political status and pursue economic, social and cultural development, while developing friendly relations with their neighbours based on respect and equal rights.

Fig. 4 Anklets for men *(arun kap)*, Ao Naga, Nagaland, latter half 19th century, goat hair, dye, vegetable fibre

Otto E. Ehlers Collection, donated in 1896 to the Royal Museum of Ethnology, Inv. No. IC28467a,b,c, Staatliche Museen zu Berlin, Ethnologisches Museum

1 The title of this article is taken from Colin Johnson's chapter, which is titled as, 'A Captured Nation: The Naga Dilemma in IWGIA', in 'The Naga Nation and Its Struggle Against Genocide', *IWGIA.org*, Copenhagen, 1986, https://www.iwgia.org/en/resources/publications/305-books/2695-the-naga-nation-and-its-struggle-against-genocide.html.

2 Franke 2009, p. 5.

3 Ibid.

4 A *sepoy* is an Indian soldier in British service. According to Makeswary Periasamy, 'Sepoys were Indian soldiers recruited from the native population of India by the European colonial power. The sepoys were trained and armed in the European manner, and were organised into battalions led by European officers.' For details see, https://eresourcep. nlb.gov.sg/infopedia/articles/SIP_1352_2008-10-30.html.

5 Ibid, p. 13.

6 Mazrui 1990, p. 244.

7 As Roy Burman says, 'the Naga conflict appears to have surfaced right after the British East India Company started flexing its politico-territorial control after defeating the Bur-mese and signing of the Yandabo Treaty in 1826.' Burman 2008, p. 147.

8 Nandita Haksar quoted in Shimray 2005, p. 15.

9 Gray 1986, p. 46.

10 Ibid.

11 Ibid, p. 47.

12 Ibid.

13 Johnson 1986 (see note 1), p. 12.

14 Ibid., pp. 14–15.

15 Dirks 2001, p. 9.

16 Ibid, p. 107.

17 Mills and Hutton were both stationed in the Naga Hills. Hutton joined the Indian Civil Service of British India in 1909 and served until 1935, while Mills joined in 1913 and served until 1947. For more details, see, http://himalaya.socanth.cam.ac.uk/collections/naga/coll/4/xintroduction/detail/all/page_2.html.

18 Gray 1986, p. 38.

19 Ibid.

20 Ibid.

21 Franke 2009, p. 7.

22 Ibid, p. 6.

23 Ibid.

24 Johnson 1986, p. 7.

25 Ibid.

26 Memorandum of the Naga Hills to the British Statutory Commission dated 10 January 1929, submitted by the Naga Club; generally referred to as the Memorandum to the Simon Commission.

27 Franke 2009, p. 39.

28 Gray 1986, p. 44.

29 Franke 2009, p. 6.

30 Ibid.

31 Johnson 1986, p. 20.

32 Nuh and Lasuh 2002, p. 115.

33 Gray 1986, p. 64.

34 Wati Aier, emeritus professor of constructive theology and philosophy, in his response to the author's questionnaire on 5 August 2020.

35 Respondent B, a Naga graduate student who requested that her name be withheld, in her response to the author's questionnaire on 6 March 2021.

36 Danspeckgruber 2002, p. 5.

37 Wohlforth and Felgenhauer 2002, p. 229.

38 Franke 2009, pp. 145–46.

39 Baruah 2003, p. 321. Also, N. K. Das says that the Naga national movement is considered 'one of the oldest unresolved armed conflicts in the world'. Das 2011, p. 70.

40 Ramunny 1988, p. 32.

41 Johnson 1986, p. 21.

42 Franke 2009, p. 1.

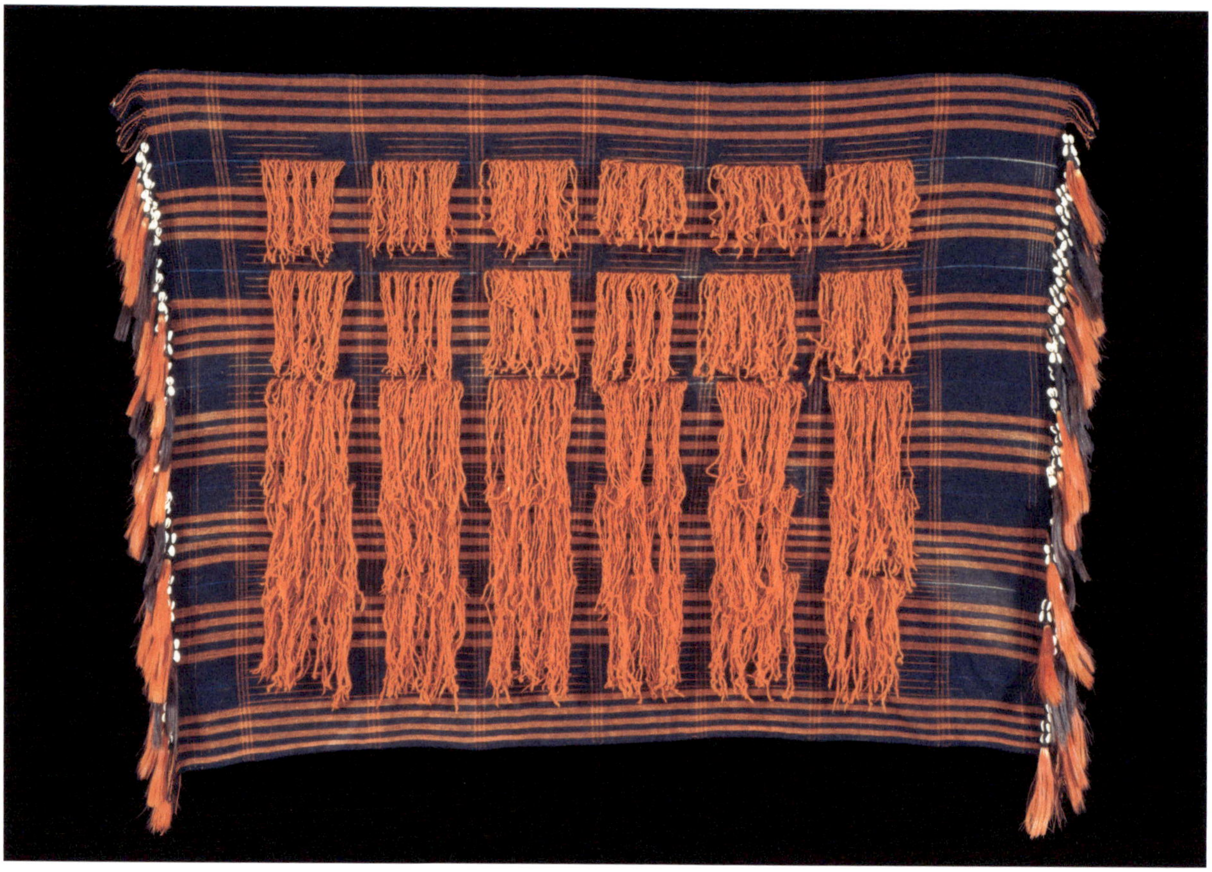

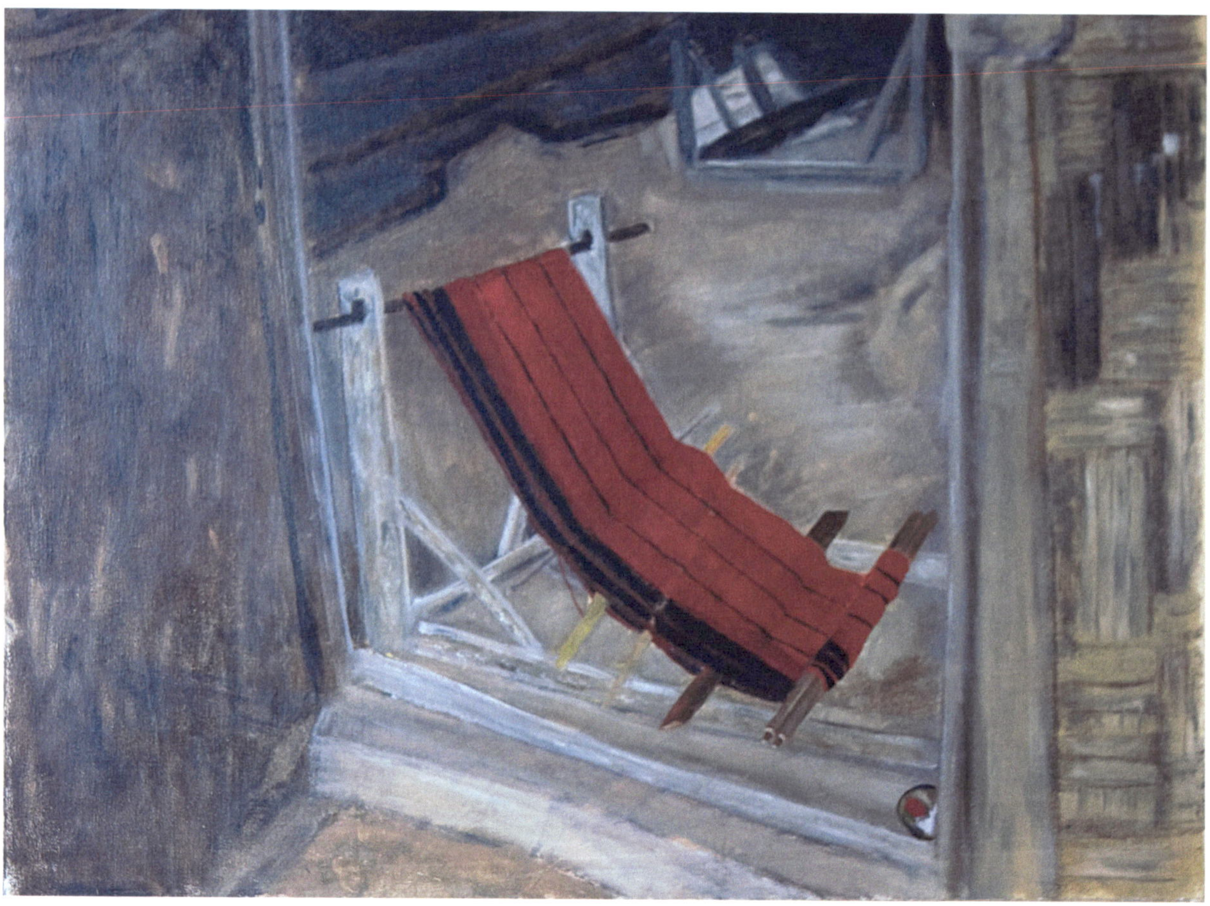

IN AND OUTSIDE MUSEUMS Reflections of an Art Historian

Iris Odyuo

In 2019, I was invited by Roland Platz from the Ethnological Museum of Berlin to have a look at the museum's Naga collection. Material culture of the Nagas exists in large numbers in Europe, the United Kingdom and the United States. The largest collections of Naga objects of around 12,000 pieces are in British museums[1] followed by the ethnological museums in Berlin, Munich and Dresden in Germany, which have about 2,000 objects collectively.[2] The Naga collections in Germany are attributed mainly to Adolf Bastian (1826–1905) and Otto Ehrenfried Ehlers (1855–1895). While such collections and studies remain precious assets, they provide little insight into those peoples' social lives.[3] In this essay, I want to reflect on some of the museum's collections and the people who made them and the transformations they are going through.[4]

STORIES THE BACK STRAP LOOM TELLS

Fig. 1 *Rongsüsü* is an Ao Naga feasts giver shawl which is richly decorated with red- and black-dyed dog's and goat's hair
Inv. No. IC 28378, Staatliche Museen zu Berlin, Ethnologisches Museum

Fig. 2 *The Loom*, 55 × 75 cm, oil on canvas, Iris Odyuo, 2007. The Loom was inspired by the story of a mother who had lost her only son in the Naga Nationalist struggle (personal communication, Tuensang, 2007)

A Chang Naga folksong, sung by the menfolk, praises the creativity of their wives in weaving the intricate patterns in the shawls which have different meanings. —
Ho … he da ah …; hai hee da ah …,
Hian doashi …, hiaa ah donyin dolen do ohh …,
Longphang jinsi dola le …

These yarns to interlace …; interlace likewise …,
Weft through the yarns interlaced, and weaves the motifs …,

DESIGNS WITH THE BEAUTY OF THE BUTTERFLIES …[5]

As an artist and researcher, I find indigenous textiles and weaving deeply inspiring. When I saw the Naga textiles in the Berlin museum, I cried out with sheer joy and relief at their pristine condition. They are preserved so well that even the natural fibres and the dyes used in making these textiles are still very vibrant. It reminded me of the ingenuity of the mothers, wives and sisters who had woven these textiles, not only for wealthy men, warriors and fallen heroes, but also for themselves and their children. It also reminded me of the many women back home who had woven textiles to fend off hunger and inhuman torture meted out to them by the Naga insurgents and the Indian armies.[6] Some of the textiles were also woven by women who had survived sexual abuses and domestic violence.[7] With a simple back strap loom[8] Naga women still preserve and create exquisite textiles, thus crafting resilience to build a better future.

CULTURAL RESILIENCE[9]

Among the exceptional collection pieces in the museum besides textiles, musical instruments, bamboo and cane baskets, ornaments and weapons et cetera are the well-known conical ceremonial hats,[10] wristlets and leg guards made of a bichromatic weave done in red-dyed cane and yellow orchid stem.

Khomong is a fifty-year-old Khiamniungan expert basket maker from Chiphur village in the Noklak district, which is some 169 kilometres from Tuensang.[11] In the 1980s, he came to Tuensang to study in the Government High School, which is now known as Tuensang Higher Secondary. He studied till class eight and took up carpentry training from the Office of Industry in Tuensang. But he soon got bored, so he went back to the village where he would observe his father and his grandfather weaving hats, wristlets and leg guards.

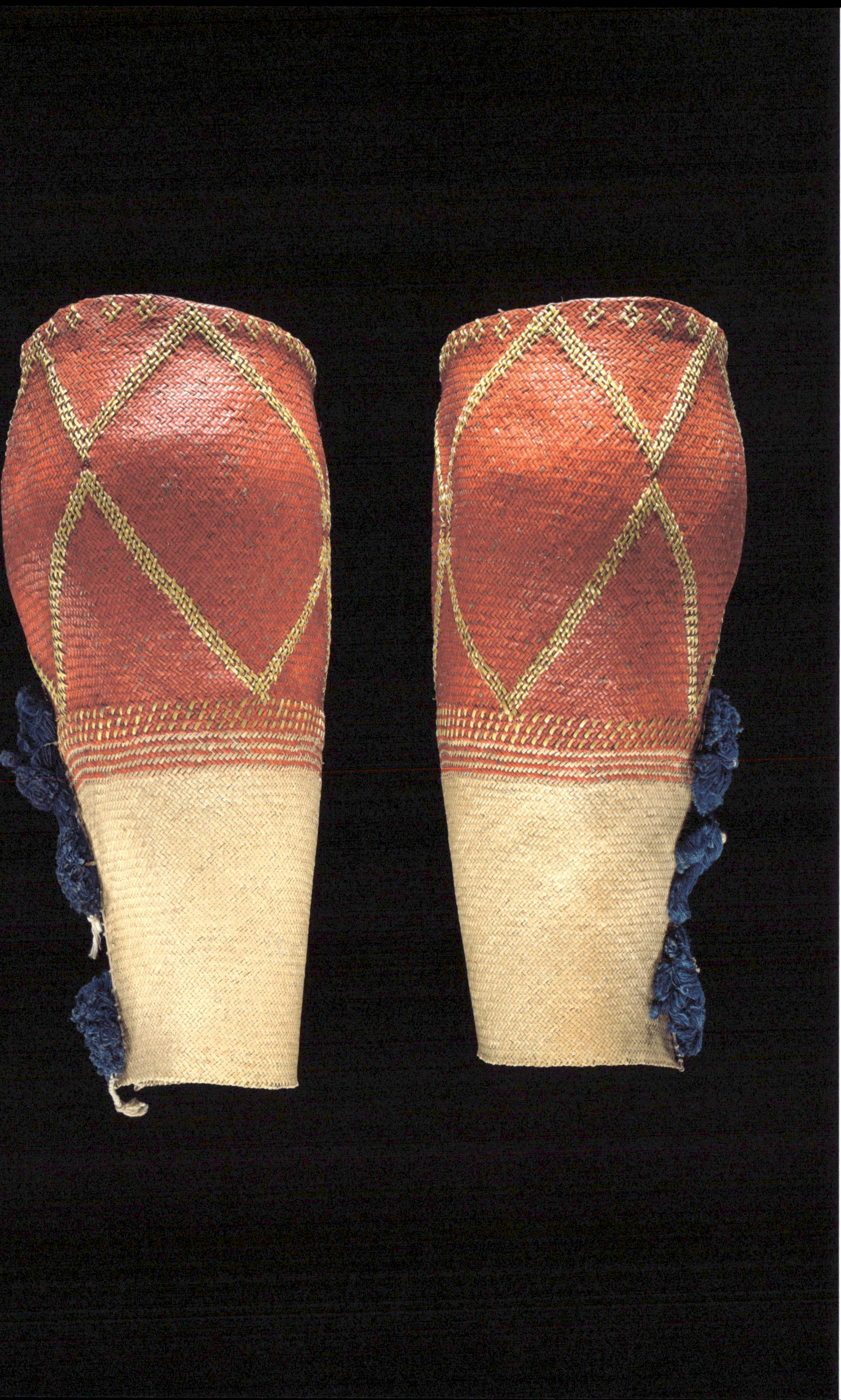

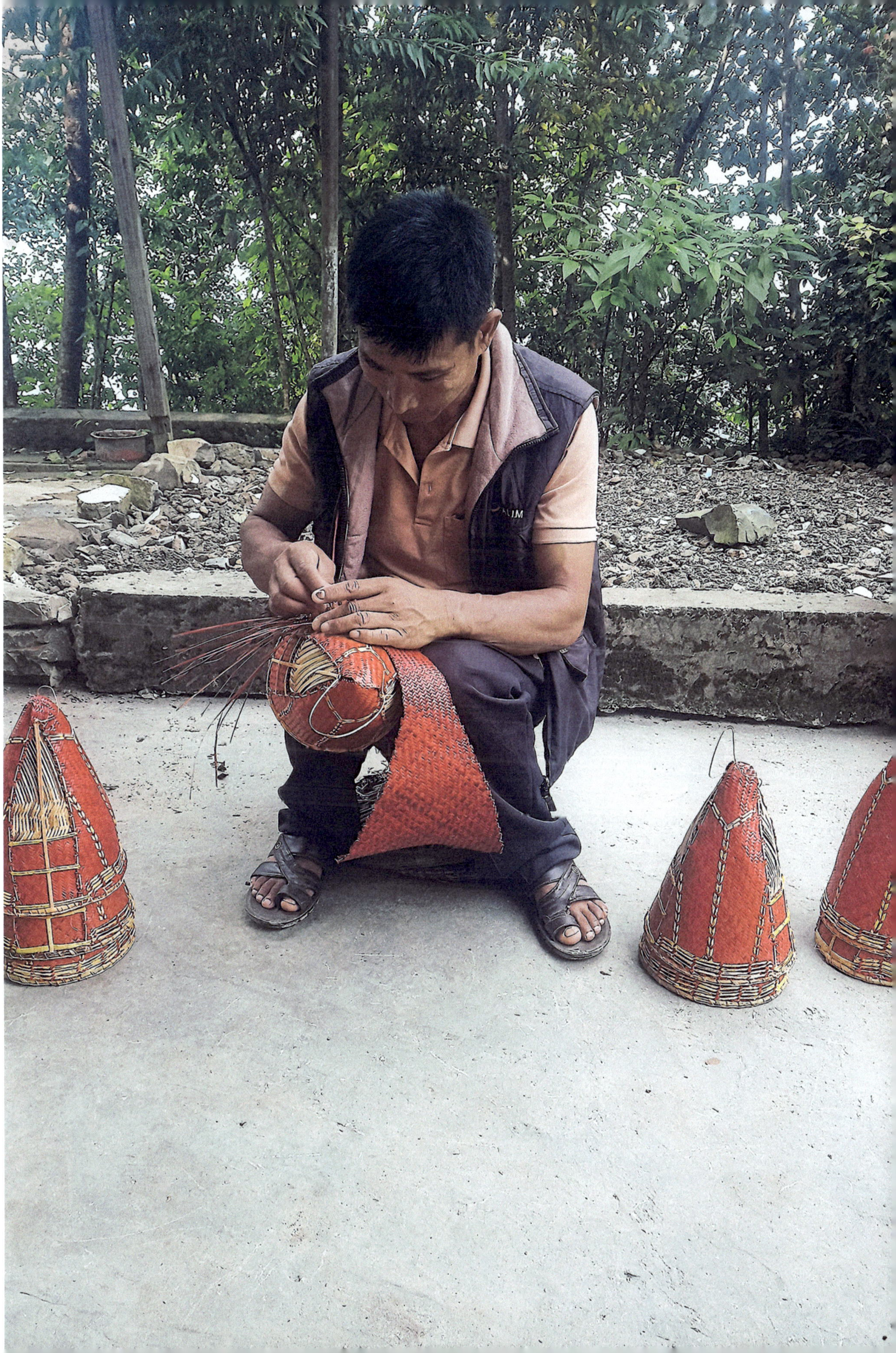

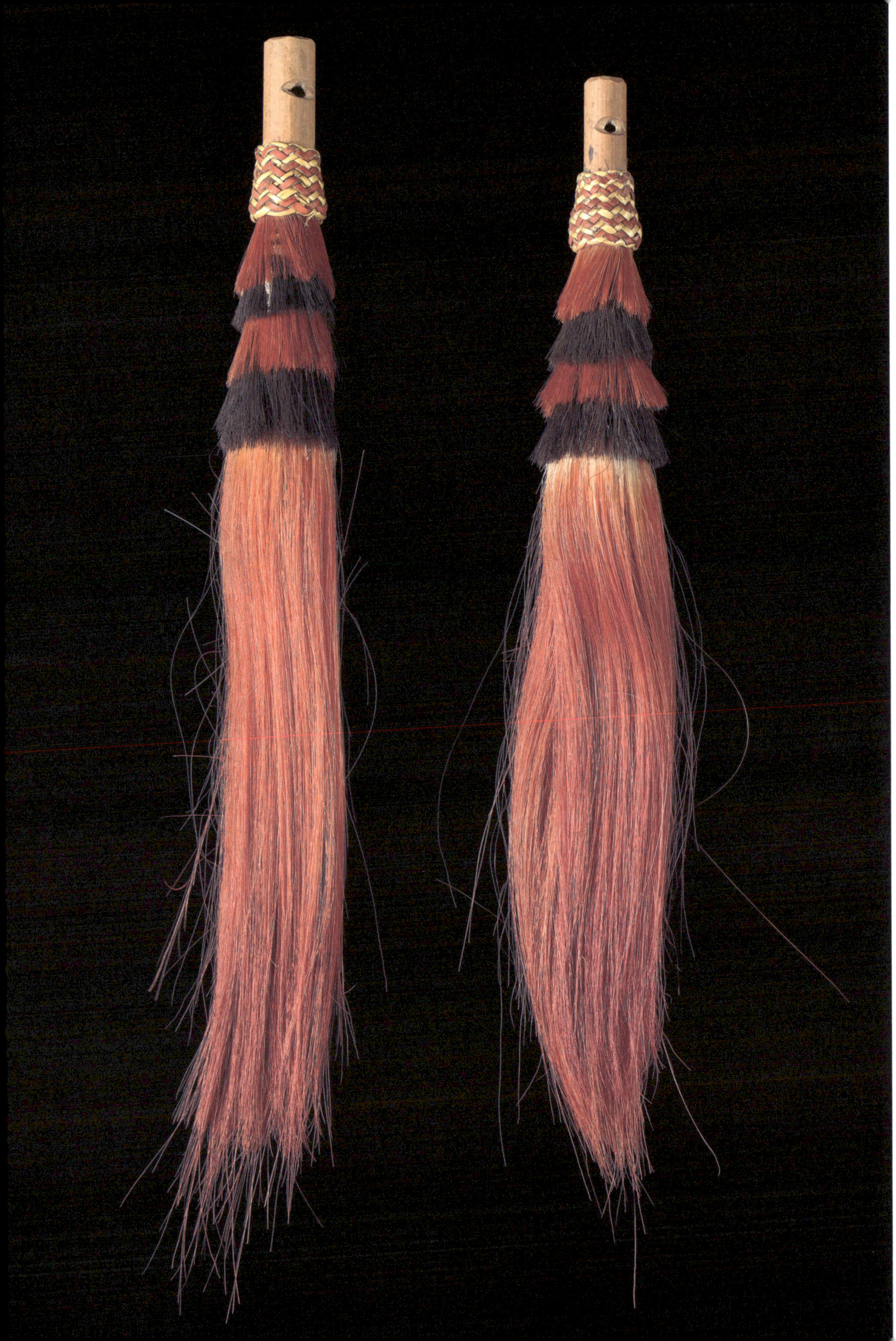

Although he could never master the complicated art of weaving the wristlets or the leg guards, he earned enough money from weaving and selling the hats to invest in a gayal (*Bos frontalis*)[12] leg for 1,500 INR (approximately 21 US dollars). He came back to Tuensang in the early 2000s and bought a plot of land and built a house, and then got married. He earns his livelihood mainly from making ceremonial has[13] but when orders from customers are low, he does masonry or carpentry work as a hired labourer. Many families who used to weave these ceremonial accessories have abandoned it, but Khomong and his father Pesing continue this traditional art. As practiced for generations, they use the same old technique of boiling the cane splints with the leaves of *haam* (no Latin or scientific name) for a week before boiling it again with the crushed bark of the *longpai* (no Latin or scientific name) tree and *wei (Rubia cordifolia)* roots.[14] Although this is a highly intensive technique, this is what gives the red-dyed cane its fastness and its lustre. He is well known in Nagaland for his intricate ceremonial accessories, such as the conical hats, wristlets and leg guards.

Fig. 3 Wristlets and legguards made of a bichromatic weave done in red-dyed cane and yellow orchid stem
Inv. No. 28111 a,b-A, Staatliche Museen zu Berlin, Ethnologisches Museum

Fig. 4 Khomong, weaving the ceremonial hat

Fig. 5 Ear plugs *(mutin)*, Konyak Naga, Wancho, Nocte (hist. Nangta Naga), Arunachal Pradesh and Nagaland, 2nd half 19th century, bamboo, hair, woven plant fibres
Otto E. Ehlers Collection, donated in 1896 by Eduard von Ohlendorff, Inv.-Nr. I C 28196 a,b, Staatliche Museen zu Berlin, Ethnologisches Museum

Fig. 6 *Numb*, 55×75 cm, oil on canvas, Iris Odyuo, 2007. "The dead hornbill symbolises the senseless killings of our braves. We see the madness all around but we prefer to remain numb." (Iris Odyuo)

Fig. 7 Hat with hornbill feathers, Ao Naga
Inv. No. IC 28388, Staatliche Museen zu Berlin, Ethnologisches Museum

HORNBILL FEATHERS IN A TIN TRUNK

It was in December 2016, while I was travelling from Tuensang to Kohima, the capital of Nagaland, in a bus, when I met a craftsman from a nearby Naga village who was going to attend the Hornbill Festival. When I inquired what he was selling at the Hornbill Festival, the biggest cultural festival in Nagaland, he said in Nagamese,[15] 'Etu saal ami khali hornbill laga puchor heh loi cha ase' (this year I am only taking hornbill feathers to sell) pointing at a shiny brand-new tin trunk underneath our seats. Every year, he takes his collections of baskets to sell at the festival, but for the past couple of years, the demand for his baskets has fallen, so he wanted to try his luck with the feathers.[16] His precious cargo soon became a curse because that particular year the selling of endangered species like the hornbill[17] was banned by a group of conservation campaigners. He has not been to the Hornbill Festival since. Despite the ban on endangered species, their sales are sometimes seen in local markets as reported in local newspapers.[18] In 2012, Pangti, a village in Nagaland, became famous for the killing of the Amur falcon (*Falco amurensis*) but by 2013, the village had become a sanctuary for the birds. This story is captured in a documentary film called *The Pangti Story* by filmmaker Sesino Yhoshu who explores how the Nagas who were culturally hunters had now become conservationists.[19] But debates about Naga food[20] according to Elspeth Iralu, a Naga scholar, overlooks the perspective that situates it in relation to other aspects of their cultural and political life. We need to recognise, she writes, 'what Nagas eat is not a sign of a barbarian past or violent present. Perhaps what Nagas eat, and our relationship to the wild and domestic animals around us, is rooted in our political context. Perhaps war, militarization and AFSPA (Armed Forces Special Powers Act)[21] affect what we eat.'[22] Extraordinary laws like the AFPSA (1958) leave the Indian armed forces with the right to kill and detain anyone throughout Nagaland and other parts of the frontier.[23] Conversations about what Nagas eat often ignore questions of militarisation, dispossession or disenfranchisement.[24]

The introduction of Christianity and mission schools not only led to the abandonment of many social and ceremonial practices connected with the traditional religions of the Nagas, but it also greatly diminished the Naga dependence and allegiance to the *morung*[25] system, the clan and the village. New forms of prestige derived from education, profession and livelihood have destroyed the prestige system that was sustaining the ceremonial art

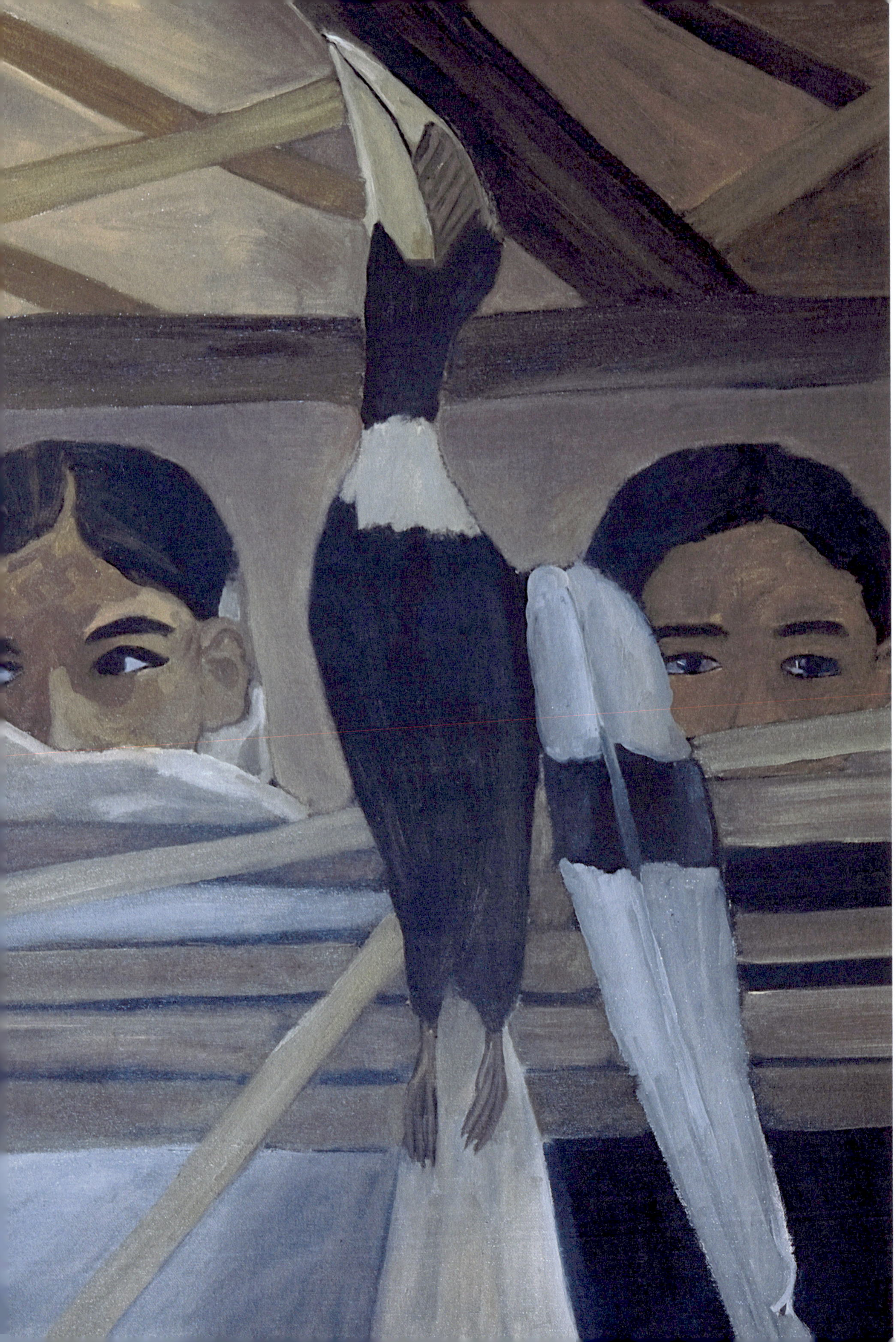

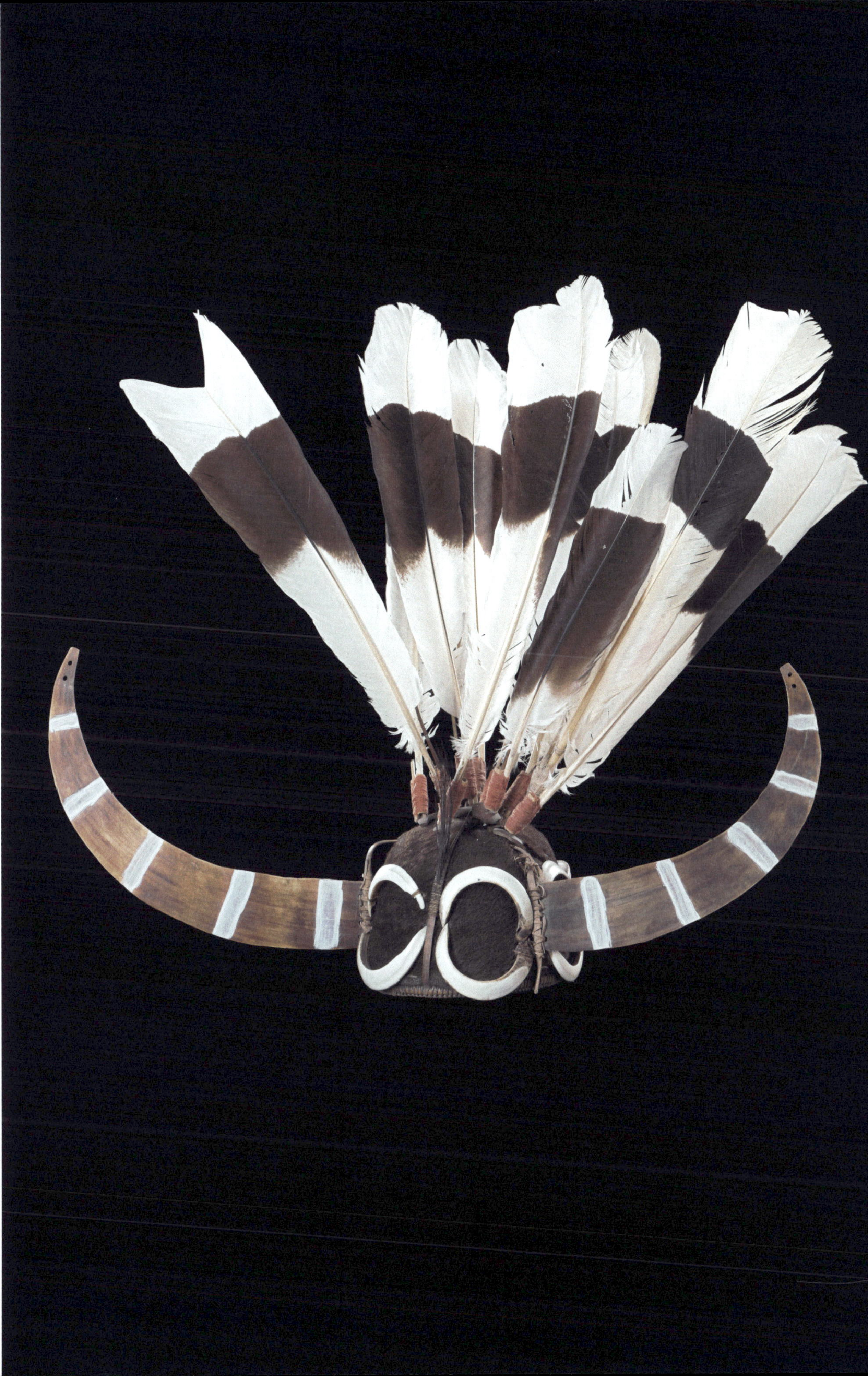

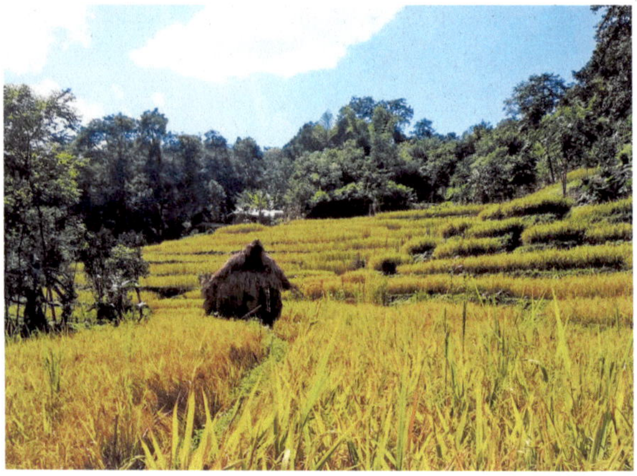

traditions. Most Naga villages destroyed their log drums[26] in the *morung*, burned or buried their traditional ornaments, and even game trophies and gayal heads stored in individual houses were abandoned. Certain traditional songs and dances invoking the blessings of the village benevolent spirits by feasts givers are considered unchristian-like and are forbidden. The destruction of cultural objects continues today; for instance, in February 2009, under the influence of the village church, the log drum and the *morung* at Bilaeshi *khel* (parts of a village inhabited by members of the same clan) in Tuensang were destroyed by the villagers themselves, as it was believed that the use of those items had led to the death of fourteen elders in the village. But according to Mülong, who had carved the log drum, the log drum had nothing to do with the dead in the village. He says that if it was so, he would have been the first one to die.[27] I narrated this story to a friend of mine, and he immediately said that he wanted to buy the log drum that was thrown away. When I asked some of the villagers if this log drum could be salvaged and bought, they replied that such an idea was ridiculous. Some of them said they would not even think of going near that log drum. That conversation made me think of introducing the villagers to the Tuensang Art and Culture Museum to help them realise the importance of their own artefacts and that they should try to preserve what they have created, but the trouble is that they lack confidence to enter the museum, not to think of appreciating the objects exhibited inside the museum. Suddenly an idea hit me: Why not go for introducing community museums,[28] a place where they can manage and collect cultural heritage themselves and tell their own stories in their own time and space, which will be instructive as well as inspiring? This would be similar to the Chumpo museum[29] at Dimapur. But that is a daunting task for me, and I will certainly need the help of the villagers. ———

TSE OÜNIÜ (THE PADDY SPIRITS)

Kongnyu, sixty-eight years old, from the village of Yokao in the Noklak district, was a very young girl when she heard the *tse* (paddy) *oüniü* (spirits) coming from the mountains and slowly floating and humming a soft enchanting sound over the ricefields and then disappearing among the rice stalks. ———

She says she had heard about them from her parents and village folk, and so she was not afraid. It is believed by the Nagas that when the *tse oüniü* come and settle in the paddy fields that there is a rich harvest. Therefore, the paddy fields are treated with respect.[30] And although there is no strict adherence to rituals and ceremonies now involved in cultivating the fields as in the old days, Naga farmers still say a prayer before trees are felled for clearing of the fields, before a new field hut is made, before a new fire is lit in the field hearth, making water channels from the mountains or rivers to bring water to the terraced rice fields and before the new seeds are sown and during and after harvest. The Chang Nagas during the *Naknyulüm* festival (festival celebrating triumph of light over darkness)[31] even pay tribute to the bamboo basket used for collecting millet known as *jeijin phoujin ownet*.[32] The winnowing basket used in sieving and gleaning rice grains or millets, mixing cooked rice with yeast for rice beer, collecting fluffed cotton balls or nettle fibres for weaving textiles, drying meat, chillies or vegetables and so on are never thrown away or burnt in the fire. They are lovingly darned and used again and again. ———

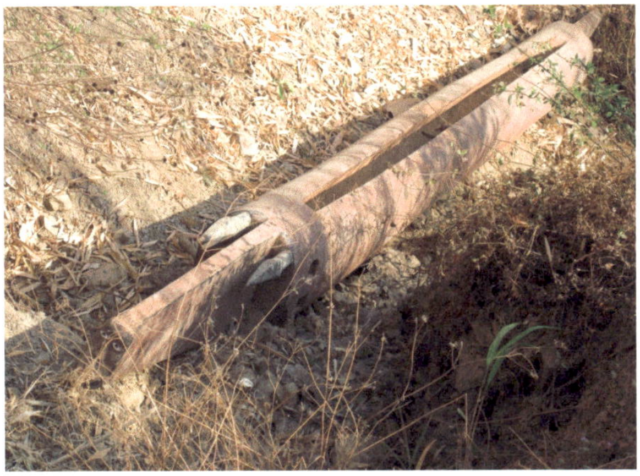

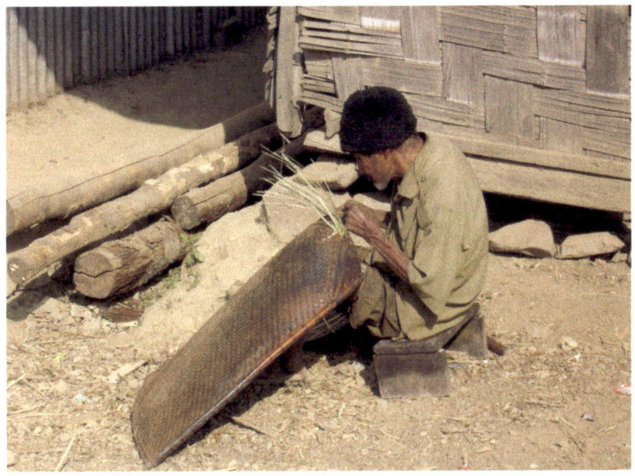

1 Macfarlane and Turin 2008.

2 Kunz and Joshi 2008.

3 Sellato 2017, p. 57.

4 Clifford 2016.

5 Chingmak Wangto 2020, p. 138.

6 See Kikon 2008 regarding the repression unleashed on the Nagas by the Indian security personnel in the early 1950s.

7 For more detailed information on women's testimonies on sexual violence, see Kikon 2015.

8 The name refers exclusively to the strap, girdle or belt which passes around the hip or waist of the weaver (Abboud 1975, p. 4). Among the Nagas, the strap was woven only by old men. Younger men were forbidden to weave the loom straps as it was believed that it would shorten their lives or that they would be killed by enemies (as told in personal communication with Khomong 2021).

Fig. 8 Terrace rice fields, Tuensang Village, 2018

Fig. 9 The Log Drum that was thrown away in Tuensang village, 2009

Fig. 10 An old man darning a winnowing basket, Tuensang Village, 2008

9 Similar to the 'cultural resilience' of the rural Kandyan communities in central Sri Lanka, some Naga arts also still rely on 'longstanding cultural traditions for their survival' (Chandima Dilhani Daskon 2010).

10 The yellow central pattern on the hat represents an abstracted tiger symbolising the spirit world as well as valour and strength. Decorations of red-dyed goat's hair and boar's tusk are added to the hat. These ceremonial accessories are only worn during festivals in the village to display wealth, prestige and prowess in war (Odyuo 2008).

11 Tuensang is one of the twelve districts of Nagaland.

12 A gayal, also called *mithun*, is an Asian bovine that is used as a rural bank for investing money. Villagers who could never afford to buy a whole gayal invest in parts of the it and sometimes end up buying the whole thing itself.

13 His conical hats are sold to handicraft shops in Tuensang, Kipheri and Dimapur.

14 See Odyuo 2008.

15 A creole language based on Assamese commonly spoken by nearly all the Naga tribes.

16 He buys the hornbill feathers from Naga villages in Myanmar, paying as much as 1,000 INR (approximately 14 USD) for a single feather. By tradition, one feather, especially the tail part, was considered equivalent to a gayal's head (Mongro 1999, p. 16).

17 The hornbill (*Dichoceros bicornis*) is greatly honoured and respected by the Nagas. It is also regarded as the king of birds. Appreciation of the magnificent appearance and graceful movements of the hornbill is expressed in their songs, textiles, woodcarvings and paintings. Most Nagas believed that the hornbill's beak and feathers represent valour and strength, and the beauty and youthfulness of the men in the village. And only a warrior and a man of wealth could wear the hornbill feathers (Odyuo 2012, pp. 117–19).

18 Nagaland Post 2018.

19 Ghosh 2018.

20 Whether it is dogs, bats or falcons? (Iralu 2021). According to N. Joseph Lemtur, the president of the Society for the Prevention of Cruelty against Animals (SPCA), it is important to recognise how the culture card is applied to legitimise certain practices, and that homogeneity is carelessly assumed among a cultural group. However, the reality is that a large number of Nagas do not eat dog meat, and many refrain from eating wild animals (Kikon 2017).

21 For more detailed information on AFSPA see Kikon 2009.

22 Iralu 2021.

23 Kikon 2017.

24 Iralu 2021.

25 The first step towards building a new village was to select the central location to construct the *morung* (men's ceremonial house). Naga villages are divided into *khels* (wards) and each *khel* has a *morung*. The *morung* was the most important social, political and religious component of the village. The numbers and size of *morung* in a village depend on its population and the vitality of the clan members who construct it. The *morung* was the centre of social and cultural life of the Nagas and had no individual existence apart from the community. It functioned as the guardhouse and armoury, recreation club, centre of education, art and discipline. It was here where debates and discussions concerning the interests of the clan and village and economic and political rituals were held and the art of warfare, and skills such as woodcarving, basketmaking, songs, dances and folklore of the tribe was communicated orally from generation to generation (Odyuo 2013, p. 16).

26 Among the Ao, Konyak, Sangtam, Phom, Chang,

Khiamniungan and the Yimchunger Nagas, the log drum is revered because it was believed that the high god who protects and blesses the village resides in it. There is a sacredness attached to the selection of the tree, the processes of construction, pulling and installation of the log drum. Among the Chang Nagas, old log drums which are replaced are never destroyed nor disposed of. The rope used in dragging the log drum was never touched by a *dao* (machete); it is carefully preserved in the *morung*. Women were not allowed to step over the towing rope of the log drum and no new carvings or paintings are done after the log drum is installed. It is only during the *Jeinyulum* festival in the month of July that further smoothing, polishing and repairs were done on the log drum (Odyuo 2012, pp. 81–82).

27 Personal communication with Mülong, *dhobashi*, Tuensang, 14 February 2009. *Dhobashis* are knowledgeable local individuals who act as intermediaries between the district administration and the villages.

28 Similar to the emergence of the consciousness of cultural loss, and hence ideas of 'saving', conservation, heritage, and the eventual embodiment of these ideas in museums among the Inuit of the central, and eastern Canadian Arctic (Graburn 2008).

29 *Chumpo* museum is a Naga model of museum and curation. Unlike traditional museums where cultures of people are frozen in cases and exhibits, a *Chumpo* museum is a living museum where the dynamism of Naga culture is an everyday lived reality (as told in personal communication with Abraham Lotha, 2010).

30 As told in personal communication, 2021.

31 *Naknyu* means 'mother of darkness' It was believed that the whole world was covered in darkness for six days and nights. During this total darkness, a hunter could not return to the village and so he took shelter in a cave. A tiger happened to pass by and the man shot it with his bow and arrow. After he killed the tiger, the darkness soon began to lift (Chingmak 2020, p. 120).

32 Chingmak 2020, p. 125.

Fig. 11 Panji basket (*soku* or *shuku*), Ao Naga, Nagaland, 2nd half 19th century, bamboo, rattan, hair, partly dyed, wood

Otto E. Ehlers Collection, donated in 1896 to the Royal Museum of Ethnology, Inv. No. IC28470, Staatliche Museen zu Berlin, Ethnologisches Museum

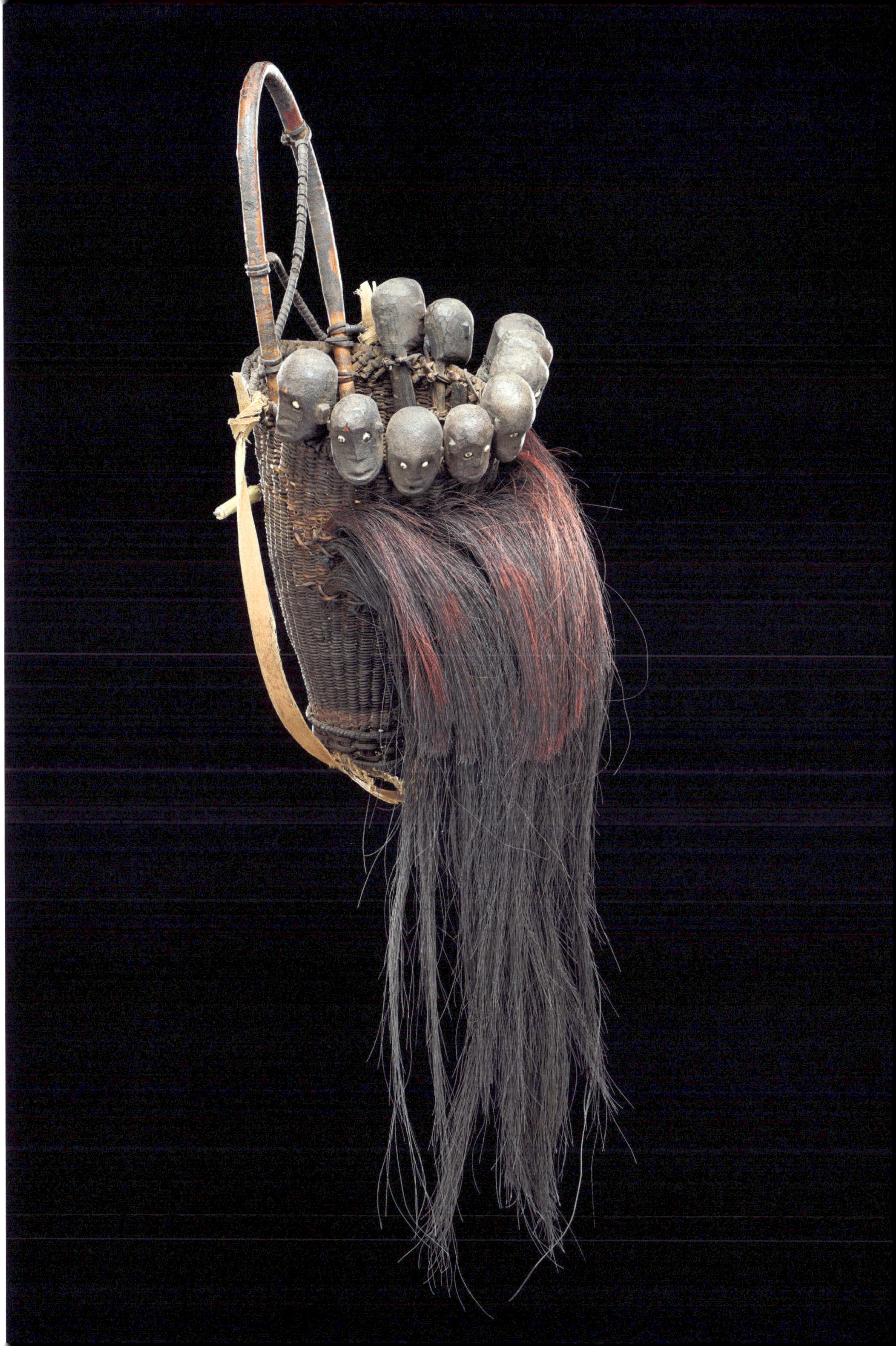

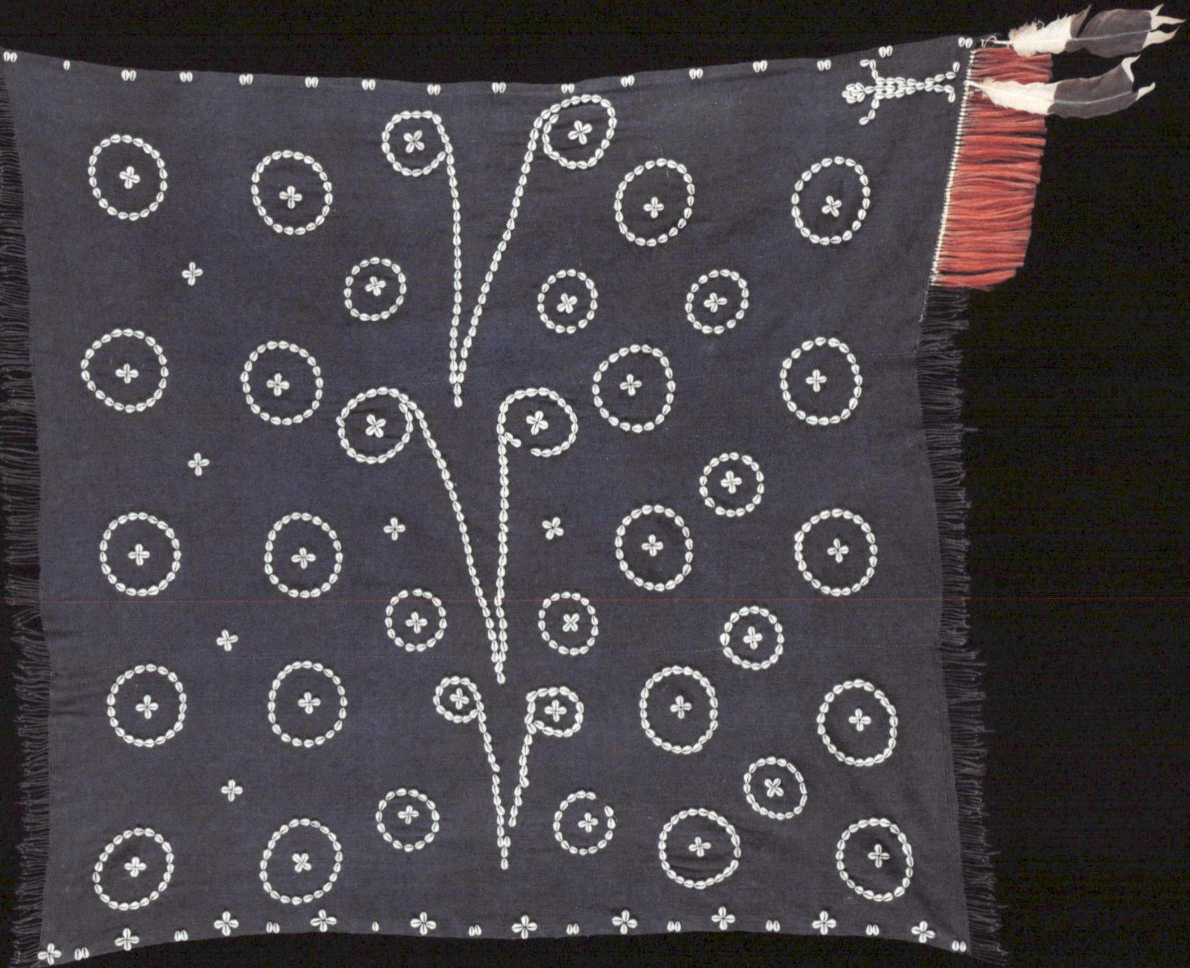

THE NAGA COLLECTION IN BERLIN AS VIEWED BY WESTERN CURATORIAL EYES

Roland Platz

The Naga are relatively unknown in Europe, in Germany at least. That was not always the case. It was not, for example, when Christoph von Fürer-Haimendorf (1909–1995), an Anglo-Austrian ethnologist, published *Die nackten Nagas* in Germany of all places in 1939. Not long afterwards the north-eastern region of India fell into a charmed slumber that lasted for over half a century. With political conflicts raging between the Indian government and Naga resistance groups, hardly anyone from abroad was allowed to travel in the region inhabited by the Naga in north-eastern India until the 1990s. Things have changed since then, but Nagaland is still not on backpackers' and travel agents' bucket lists. The regional infrastructure is still too creaky, which makes travel there genuinely challenging.

In 2008, *Naga: A Forgotten Mountain Region Rediscovered*, an exhibition mounted by the Museum der Kulturen in Basel, proved a hit with visitors. Quite a few of the exhibits came from the Ethnological Museum collection in Berlin. It is not just Naga society as such that is fascinating, but also the artefacts from it, particularly those dating from the nineteenth and early twentieth centuries. The word 'fascinating' has been deliberately used here, in full awareness of its exoticising connotations. It doesn't take much to be enchanted with cloth featuring luminous reds on indigo-blue grounds, helmet crests of red-dyed goat hair, all of them imaginatively and individually designed, or to be intrigued by decorations fashioned from the shells of cowries and other molluscs, orchid stalks, boar tusks and tiger fangs.

Fig. 1 Warrior's cloth (*jihussi*), Ao Naga, Nagaland, latter half 19th century, cotton, woven, cowrie shells, dyed hair, hornbill feathers

Otto E. Ehlers Collection, donated in 1896 to the Royal Museum of Ethnology, Inv. No. IC28378a, Staatliche Museen zu Berlin, Ethnologisches Museum

The Naga collection in Berlin is one of the oldest of its kind anywhere. The first objects were acquired as long ago as 1878 although most went to the Königliche Museum für Völkerkunde, as the Berlin Ethnological Museum was then called, in the 1880s. Parts of the museum collection, and this is also true of a part of the Naga collection, were carried off to the Soviet Union in 1945 after the end of the Second World War. Hundreds of Naga objects were returned to Berlin via the Leipzig Grassi Museum in 1991–92. Some 700 artefacts, including carvings of a kind no longer represented in the collection, have, however, vanished.

DISTINGUISHED COLLECTORS: SAMUEL E. PEAL

Samuel Edward Peal (1834–1897), a British collector, was particularly important for the creation of the Berlin Naga collection. According to the inventory log and the Ethnological Museum digital database, only sixty objects are officially credited to him, yet the assistance he was able to give to the German collectors Adolf Bastian and Otto E. Ehlers through good contacts to the Naga, was crucial. A significant part of the Ehlers collection may have originally been acquired from Peal. Be that as it may, the Peal objects were donated to the Berlin Museum in 1896 along with most of the Ehlers Collection by Eduard von Ohlendorff, who had inherited the artefacts from Ehlers.

By the 1860s, Peal had undertaken expeditions to the Naga settlement area and had also acquired objects there. It is unclear whether any objects in the Berlin Museum date from that era.

Peal was an artist, tea planter and keen amateur botanist, who discovered the cause of the mildew that attacked tea plants. He

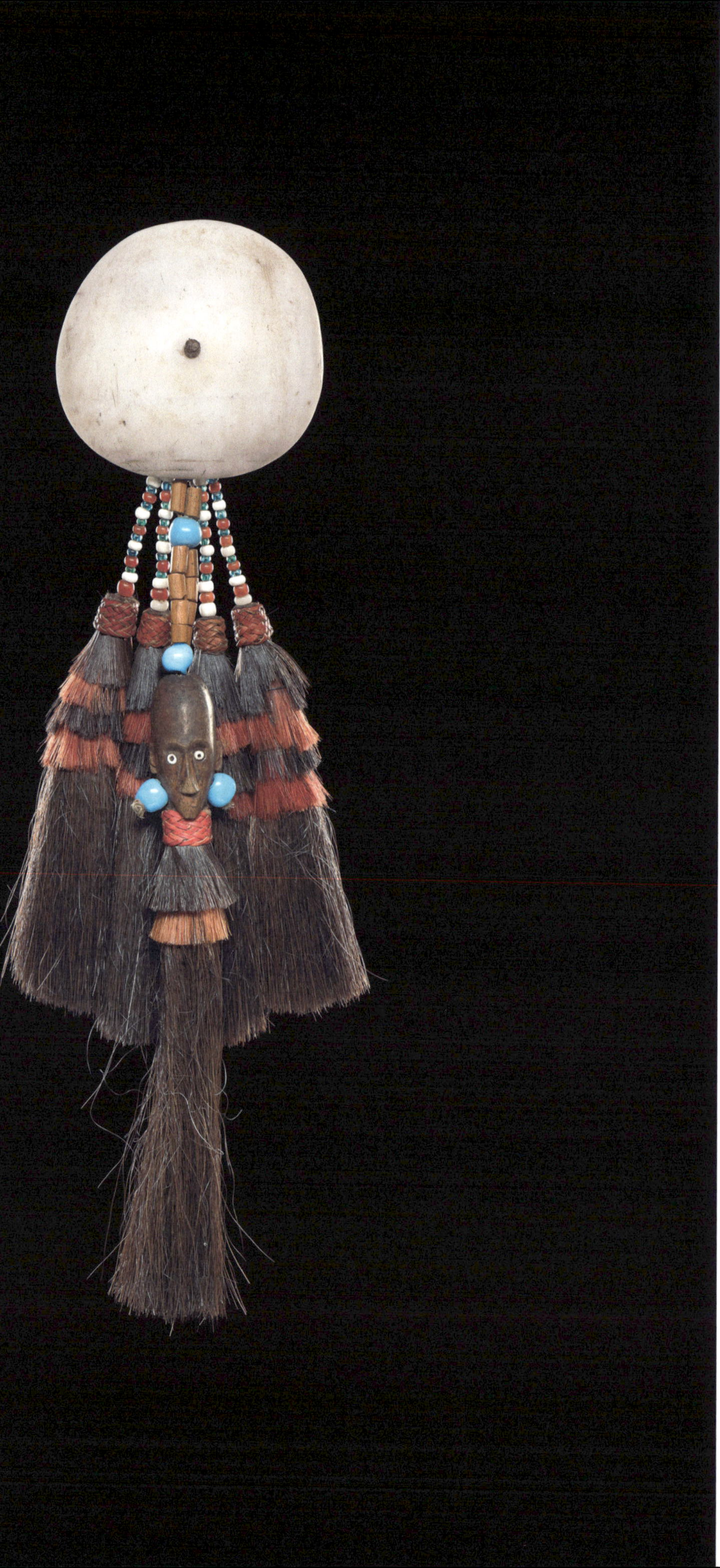

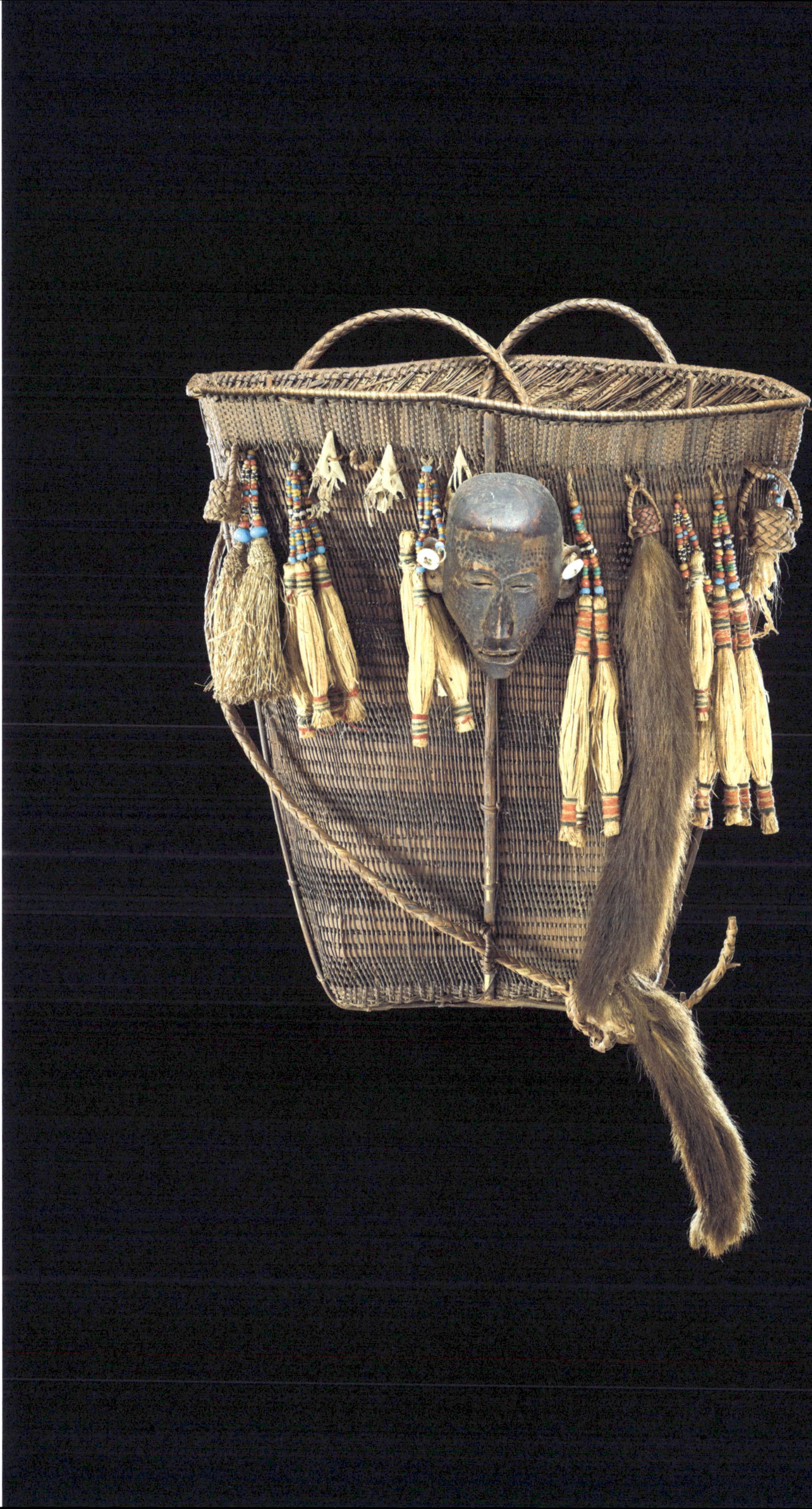

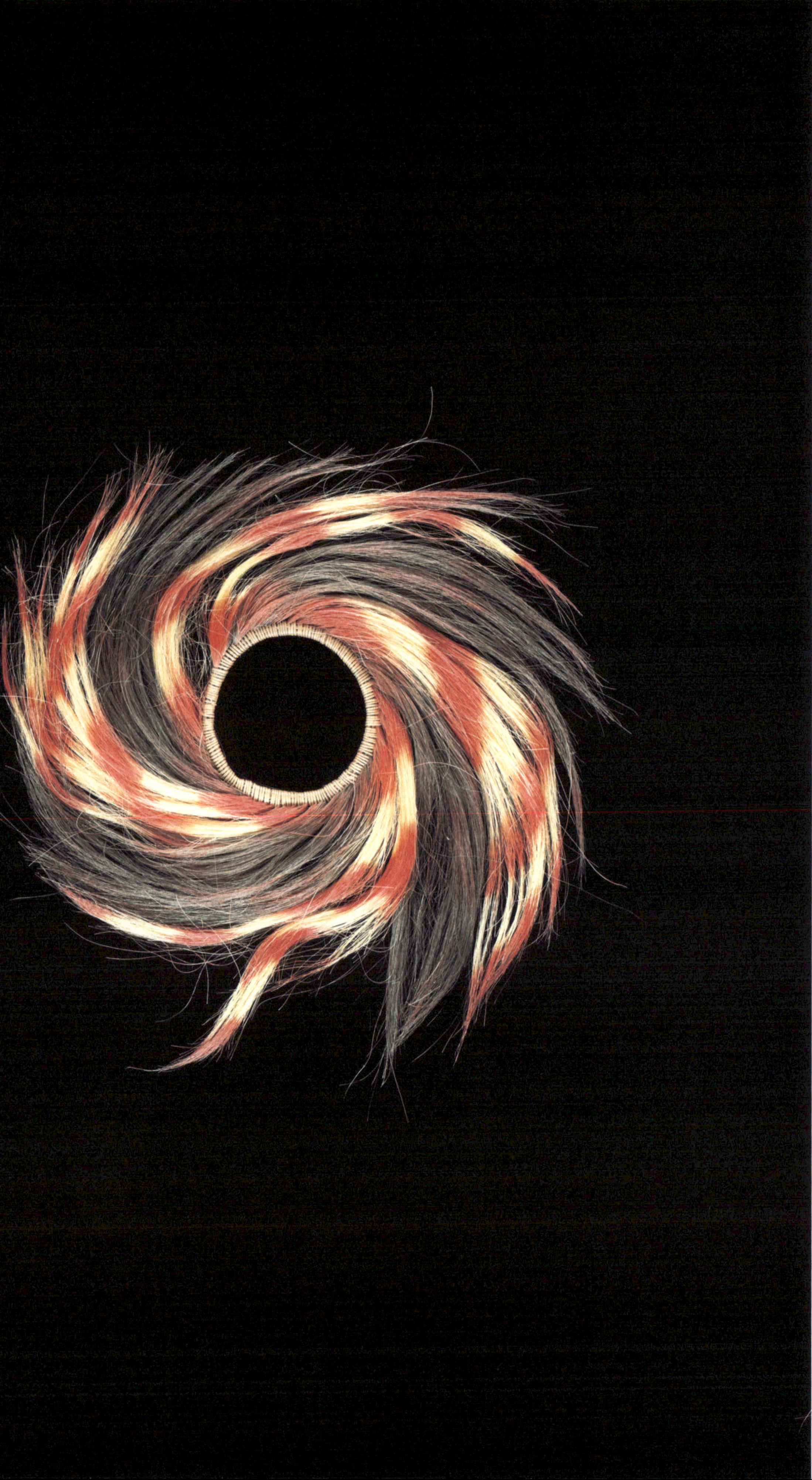

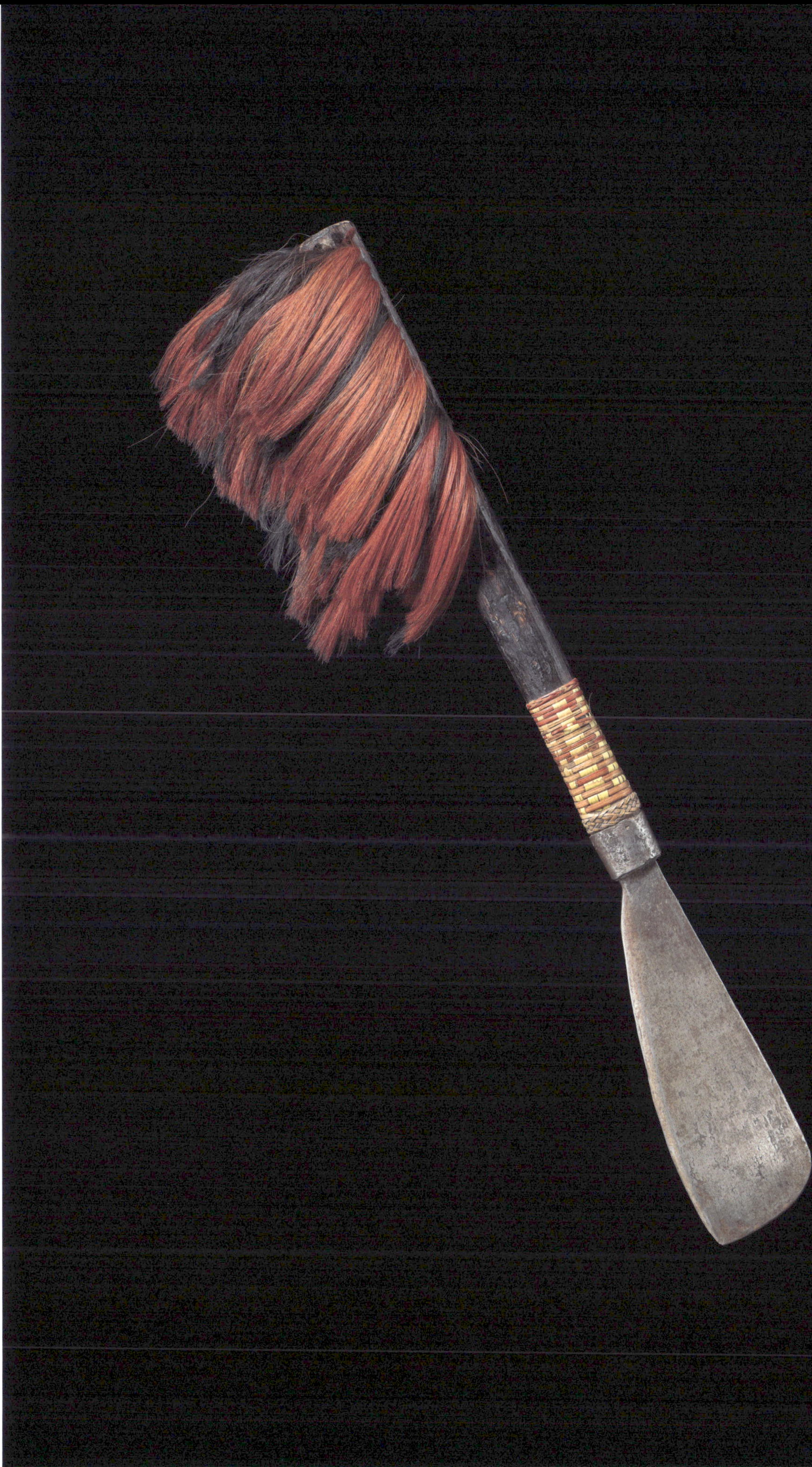

was also interested in ethnology and was one of the first explorers to write reports on the Naga. In 1862, he went as a tea planter to Sivasagar (Sibsagar) in what is now the state of Assam. His travels took him to regions that had never really been brought under British control by the time British colonial rule ended in 1947. Peal had contacts to Naga individuals for many years. In 1868, he went on a small expedition, accompanied by a German explorer, two overseers, two policemen and a translator as well as two pack elephants, to the Naga groups living in what is now Assam and Arunachal Pradesh. He had been invited to the area by the village chieftain of Banpara. The groups living there now call themselves Wancho, but are closely affiliated with the Konyak Naga.

Peal's travel diary, entitled *Notes of a Visit to the Tribes Inhabiting the Hills South of Sibsagar, Asam* [sic], reached the library of the Berlin Society for Anthropology via Heinrich Blochmann, secretary of the Asiatic Society of Bengal in Calcutta (now Kolkata). It contains portraits Peal painted of Naga as well as maps and botanical drawings. Translated into German by the Indologist Kurt Klemm, the Peal travel diary was published in 1898 in the *Zeitschrift für Ethnologie*.[1] In it, Peal describes encounters with Naga: 'The expedition had their men unpack what they had brought with them. They had known in advance that the intended recipients would be dissatisfied with the offerings, or at least would pretend to be, as their custom was. For the Raja (the village headman) a grand purple robe with broad strips of silver braid, a scarlet shirt and some penknives, a red blanket and 20 rupees in cash.'[2]

Rifles, which the Naga would have preferred, were denied them. This gives us an inkling of how Peal, and later the Ethnological Museum, came to own some of the objects. Donation, purchase and exchange are the usual acquisition channels. However, Peal seems to have built up a relationship with the Naga based on mutual trust.

ADOLF BASTIAN

Adolf Bastian (1826–1905), physician, ethnologist and collector, founded the Berlin Völkerkundemuseum. His extensive travels took him to what are now India and Myanmar, and he stayed in British colonial India for months at a time. In 1878, he set out from Sibsagar in Assam to the Naga Hills, where he was invited by Edward Clark and his wife, Mary Mead Clark, American Baptist missionaries, to visit the first Naga village to have converted to Christianity, Molungkimong, inhabited by Ao Naga.[3]

Bastian must have also met Samuel E. Peal then, although no encounter is noted in Bastian's published account of the expedition. In an article from 1881 Bastian wrote for the *Zeitschrift für Ethnologie* and in his book on *Völkerstämme am Brahmaputra* (1883), he describes religious observances, social relations and headhunting among the Naga but fails to mention personal encounters, not even with Naga. Bastian acquired 700 objects, of which 176 survived. It is unclear whether Peal or others had a hand in procuring those artefacts or whether most were obtained through the village of Molungkimong. Unfortunately, nothing is known about how the objects came into Bastian's possession.

OTTO E. EHLERS

Otto Ehrenfried Ehlers (1855–1895), adventurer extraordinaire, collector and travel writer, read law and acquired an estate in Pomerania before travelling in the 1880s through Africa and later also Asia. Most of the Berlin Naga collection was acquired by him. Commissioned by Bastian to enlarge the Naga collection, Ehlers travelled to Manipur in 1890, and to Assam in 1893, 1894 and 1895. He reached the same region as Peal before him, home to the eastern, or 'naked' Naga[4] (Nangta), and now inhabited by Konyak Naga, Wanchos and Nocte. From

Fig. 2 Ear jewellery for men (*tok muniyak*), Konyak Naga, Wancho, Nocte (hist. Borduaria), Nagaland or Arunachal Pradesh, latter half 19th century, shells, hair, dye, vegetable fibre, glass beads, wood

Otto E. Ehlers Collection, donated in 1896 to the Royal Museum of Ethnology, Inv. No. IC28340a, Staatliche Museen zu Berlin, Ethnologisches Museum

Fig. 3 Warrior's basket, Naga, north-east India, latter half 19th century, bamboo, vegetable fibres, pelt, bird bill

Charles Dowding Collection, sold in 1896 to the Royal Museum of Ethnology, Inv. No. IC27981, Staatliche Museen zu Berlin, Ethnologisches Museum

the Namtzik (now Wancho?) Ehlers acquired the first collection to be brought to Europe. Ehlers collected more than 1,600 objects altogether for the Berlin Museum, including artefacts from the Wancho, Nocte, Abor, Mischmi and Daphla, who are no longer regarded as belonging to the Naga.[5]

Well known as a travel writer, Ehlers gave an account of his adventures in Manipur in his book *An indischen Fürstenhöfen* (1894). In 1895, Ehlers was shot dead by indigenous members of his expedition in Kaiser-Wilhelms-Land, now Papua New Guinea.

Most of the Ehlers collection was donated to the Museum in 1896 by Eduard, Baron von Ohlendorff, from the Mecklenburg estate Gut Gresse, which he had inherited on Ehlers' death.

Here, too, the acquisition route is murky. Objects were bought, acquired by barter, sometimes given as presents or simply discarded because converts to Christianity were pressured by missionaries to part from possessions, even mundane objects. It is quite safe to assume that none of these objects came from punitive expeditions engaged in by the British against recalcitrant villages that refused to submit to colonial rule or infringed British colonial laws enacted against headhunting. On such military operations, known as 'punitive expeditions', objects were also stolen that later ended up in British museums.

In general, however, the Naga had a relatively high degree of autonomy: large parts of the region they inhabited were never under British control. German collectors were supported on their acquisition forays by British colonial officials.

The National Museum in Kohima, the capital of Nagaland State, houses a collection of artefacts, some of them quite old, yet dating from a more recent period than those in the Berlin Ethnological Museum. Otherwise, there are virtually no objects in Nagaland that are more than thirty or forty years old. The reasons for this are that prices have skyrocketed on the art market and, above all that, Christianisation of the Naga set in with renewed vigour during the 1970s. Many objects were destroyed or discarded because they were viewed as the devil's handiwork.

Viewed from the Western curatorial standpoint, the Berlin collection is superb. On the one hand, these historic pieces are no longer available; on the other, hardly anyone now possesses the skills needed to make such artefacts. Exhibitions devoted to the material culture of the Naga usually meet with enormous enthusiasm on the part of Western visitors. The loss of skills applies to basket weaving, a craft practised by men, and weaving textiles, the domain of women, who are responsible for what are often complicated patterns. Nonetheless, the tradition of textile and basket weaving continues to be upheld, often, however, with new materials and designs. New objects have been deliberately integrated in the current exhibition at the Humboldt Forum to demonstrate that there is continuity along with change in textiles and jewellery making. The 'old' is not necessarily preferred to the 'new'; quite the contrary, it's often the other way round. Although patterns, techniques and materials have changed, the quality of newly woven textiles is nevertheless high, and this is appreciated. New textiles are often worn on special occasions. Western clothing has, of course, found its way into everyday life. No society is static, and the Western perspective often applies aesthetic standards to an artefact that differ from those brought to bear on it by the society in which it originated.

What would be the best approach for the Ethnological Museum to adopt in dealing with its collection of historic artefacts? Collaboration with several academic institutions in Nagaland is planned for the future. Avid interest in the proposal was indicated in talks that took place in Dimapur, Nagaland, in 2018. The objects concerned are to be made digitally available for use by all parties involved to facilitate further research. The fact

Fig. 4 Arm ring for men (*dahpan*), Konyak Naga, Wancho, Nocte (hist. Namsangia Naga), Nagaland or Arunachal Pradesh, latter half 19th century, goat hair, dye, vegetable fibre

Otto E. Ehlers Collection, donated in 1896 to the Royal Museum of Ethnology, Inv. No. IC28296, Staatliche Museen zu Berlin, Ethnologisches Museum

Fig. 5 Ritual machete (*dao*), Naga, Nagaland, latter half 19th century, low-carbon steel alloy, dyed hair, wood

Otto E. Ehlers Collection, donated in 1896 to the Royal Museum of Ethnology, Inv. No. IC28009, Staatliche Museen zu Berlin, Ethnologisches Museum

there is an old collection of artefacts representing the Naga material culture in Berlin is still largely unknown in Nagaland. It is, however, up to the Naga to decide whether the objects are part of their cultural legacy or not. A situation observed during a brief research stay in Nagaland in 2014 is interesting in this regard. Most villagers there tended to prefer objects in their possession that dated from much more recent periods. Hitherto, it has been mainly scholars from Nagaland who have been aware of their unique material culture. An exhibition in Nagaland is a desideratum, yet it would need venues that are suitably climate-controlled. Residency programmes that would enable artists and scholars from Nagaland to stay in Berlin and conduct research at the museum are also in the pipeline. Collaboration with the art photographer Zubeni Lotha as co-curator of this exhibition at the Humboldt Forum is a first step towards a prospective partnership of this kind, and the outlook is promising. ————

1 First published in Peal 1872.

2 Klemm 1898, p. 332: the quotation from the German translation is paraphrased here.

3 In Bastian's notes the village is called Mailum (Bastian 1881). That place name was used in the Museum inventory log. Now the Ao-Naga village is called Molungkimong. The village from which Molungkimong, later a Christian settlement, originally split off was known as Deka-Haimon.

4 They were called 'naked Nagas' because both men and women often wore nothing but scant loincloths.

5 The term 'Naga' is a political concept. Groups in neighbouring Indian states who are culturally affiliated with the Naga in Nagaland do not tend to call themselves Naga, whereas that was the name used for them by the British in the colonial era.

Fig. 6: Ear jewellery *(muniak)*, Konyak Naga, Wancho, Nocte (hist. Namsangia), Nagaland or Arunachal Pradesh, 2nd half 19th century, hair, dye, glass beads, plant fibres

Otto E. Ehlers Collection, donated in 1896 to the Royal Museum for Ethnology, Inv. No. I C 28292a,b, Staatliche Museen zu Berlin, Ethnologisches Museum

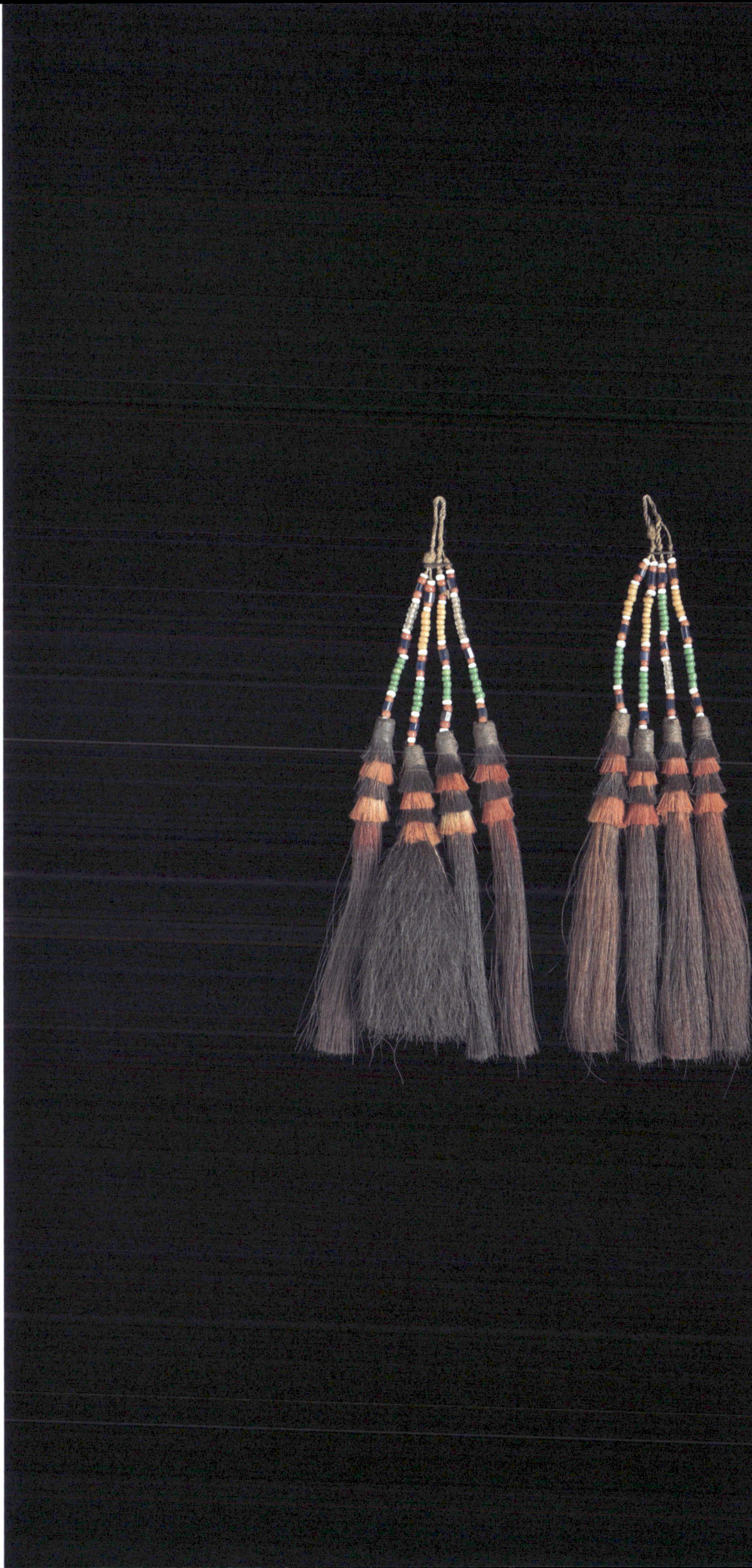

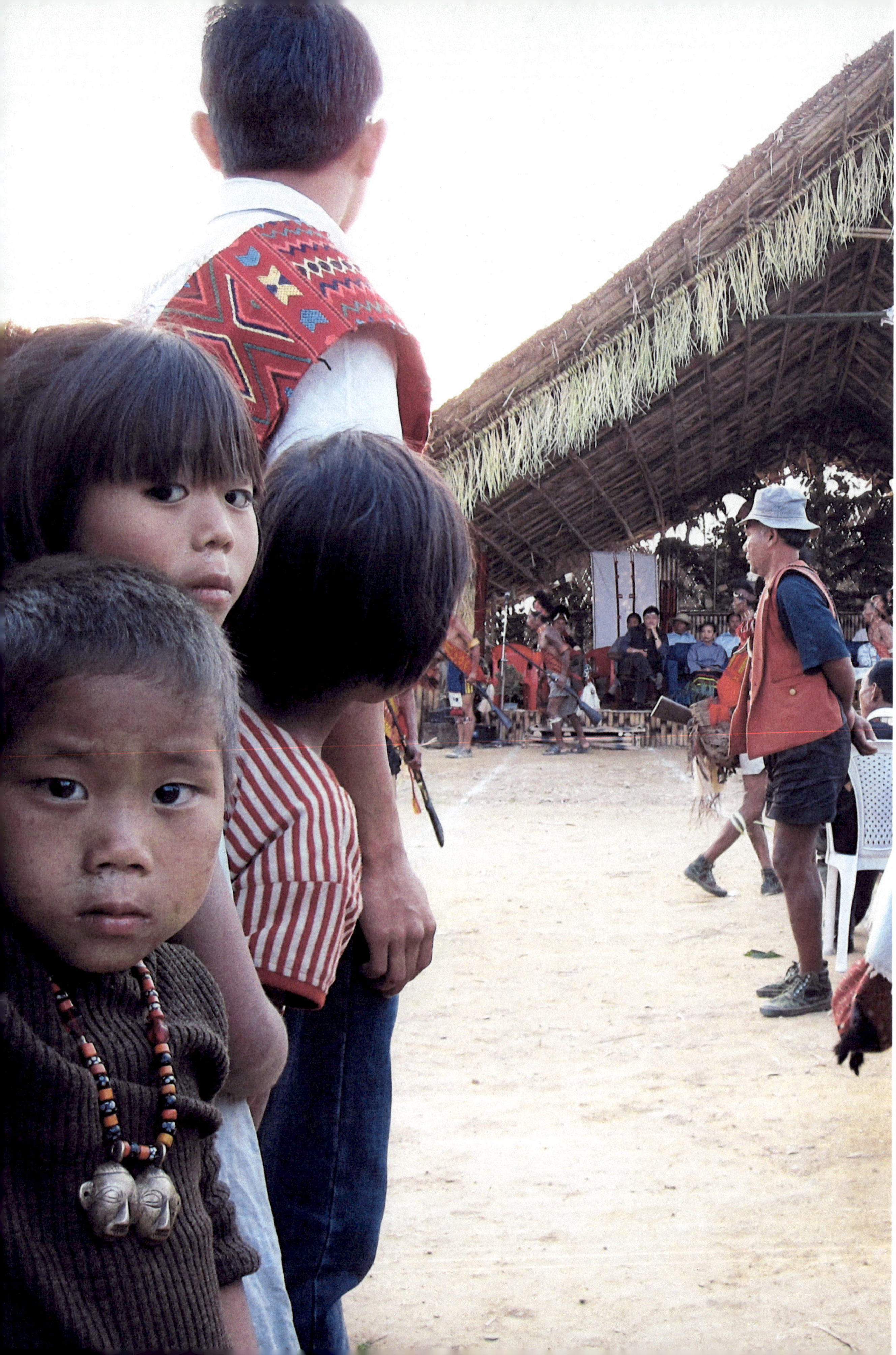

PRESENT DAY NAGA SOCIETY A Story about Culture

Dolly Kikon

If you are interested in Naga culture, it is impossible to skip the Konyak people and the Mon district. When I was doing my doctoral fieldwork along the foothills of Assam and Nagaland, I met workers in the Naga coal mines. Unplanned and entirely as an impulsive decision, I ended up in the district headquarters, Mon town. I come from the Lotha tribe and have no kin connection with the Konyak tribe. However, the Lotha tribe and the Konyak tribe identify themselves as part of the larger Naga nation, the Naga people. This allowed me to feel at home in the Mon district. This essay presents my anthropological reflections about my time in the Mon district.

I arrived in Mon town and, like many visitors, I was there to attend the Mon Road Show cum Aoleang Festival in 2010. We were surrounded by vibrant colours, warriors, dancers and the sounds of jubilant laughter. The presence of important state officials and the Chief Minister of Nagaland, Neiphiu Rio, for the festival meant the air was filled with expectation and excitement. As a doctoral student conducting fieldwork in Nagaland, I did not carry any curriculum or guidebook about Naga culture with me to travel to the Mon district. The district is marked with bad roads and there is an absence of basic infrastructure, like health care and education, which have forced young people to become migrants and leave their villages. Poverty has forced Konyak children from their villages and across the districts of eastern Nagaland to become domestic maids in Naga households.[1]

Fig. 1 Children of Chi village watching a warrior dance performance

If you ever find yourself in Mon, you are either a tourist chasing Naga culture or a government official posted in the remote district. Nevertheless, 2010 in the district was unlike any other year. Naga culture stuck to you like your best friend. It demanded all your strength and attention, and tired you out. The entire chain of mountain villages prepared to adorn themselves with banners and new bamboo podiums erected on village playgrounds to welcome the Chief Minister of Nagaland and a stream of accompanying visitors. The images in the essay are from my doctoral fieldwork of that time. If you were in the audience like me, the state played an integral role in producing and teaching what ought to be Naga culture.

What is official culture as opposed to living culture, then? This question began to shape my understanding of what Naga society determines and attributes as Naga culture. Collapsing what is being recorded and what is left out or edited because it is out of sync, I began to focus on 'out-of-place' or 'taken-forgranted' moments to explore how Naga culture is produced through everyday experiences and lived realities. The comparisons denoting authenticity and a treasured past take place, in many cases, by reproducing cultural motifs in woven fabric, jewellery or a mishmash of colours, sounds and stories from the past. I grew up with songs, designs and events that were never recorded in the past as Naga culture but played a vital role in shaping my life as a Naga. For me, the brilliance of exceptional things about being a Naga begins with the realisation that *deep engagement* emerges only when we move away from *perfect* moments of Naga culture and society. To recognise and learn from the unexamined lives that are cut out from the coffee table books and postcards on Naga culture, a template that is often adopted to exoticise Naga people, is precisely when real education and connection to Naga culture starts. For me, the education began by demonstrating responsibility to land, to each other and to be accountable to the future Naga generations through capturing what the official culture deems unaesthetic and unsightly.

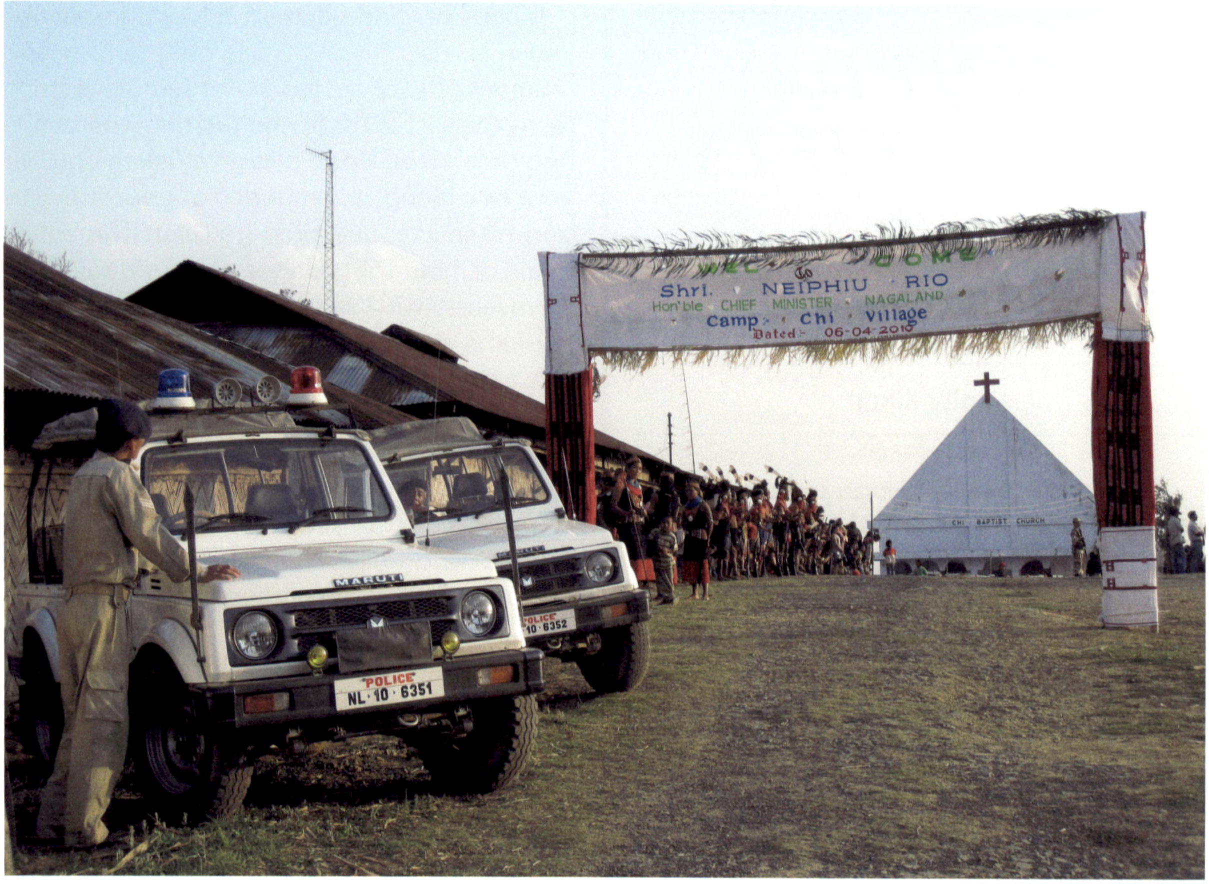
Shri. NEIPHIU RIO
Hon'ble CHIEF MINISTER NAGALAND
Camp:- Chi Village
MARUTI
POLICE
NL·10·6351

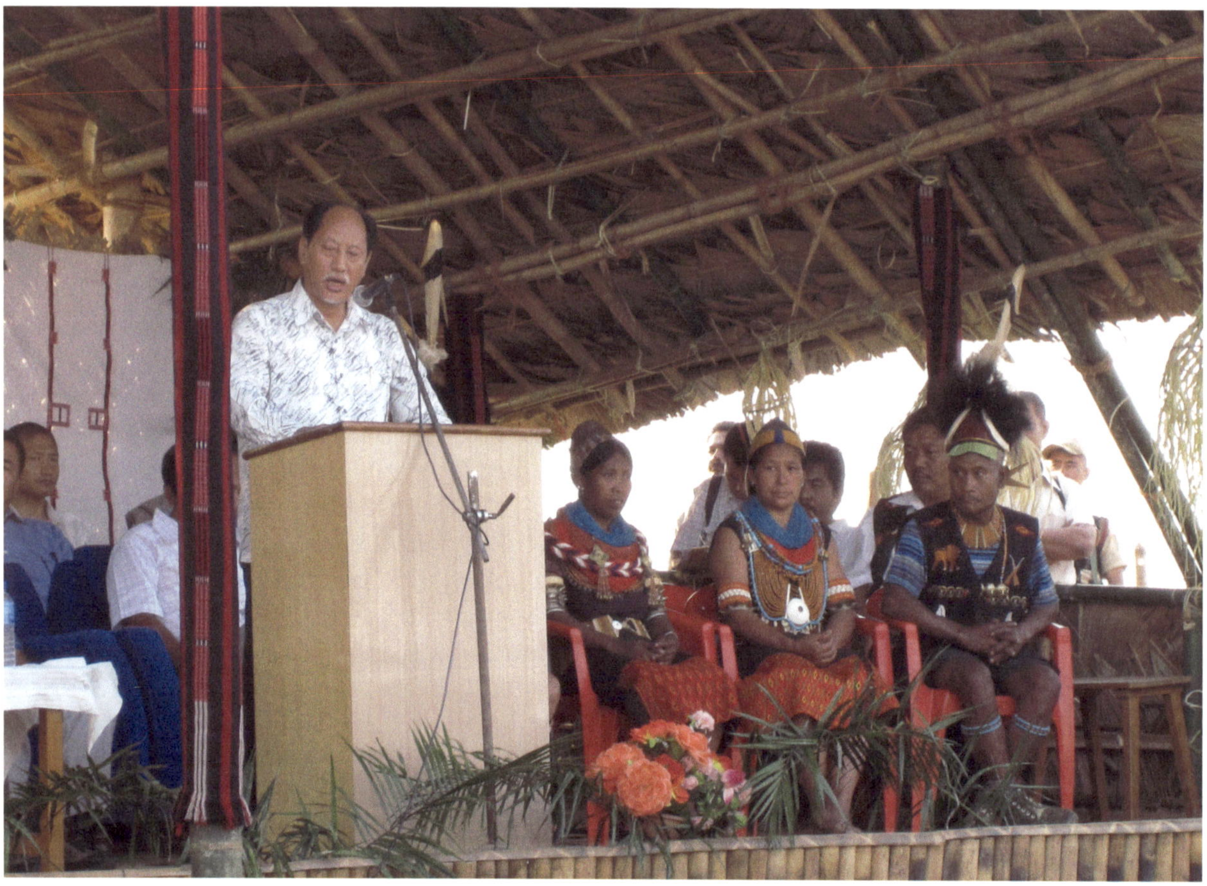

My field reflections, I hope, allow us to understand contemporary Naga culture and society. One of the most studied communities in British India, the Naga people and their lives were seen through a colonial gaze, which decontextualised and devalued the Naga ways of life. Naga culture today is not limited to fabric, dance, song or text. What is it, then? Critiquing the quest for an authentic experience of Naga culture, the images in this essay present insights into the diversity of meanings and values that are generated on the ground in contemporary Naga society. I categorise the photographs as a collective Naga experience that constitutes what I refer to as a living Naga culture founded on practice and engagement. Originating from the land, situated in the lives of individuals and communities, negotiating structures of power and authority, Naga society continuously seeks to balance existing relationships and connections. Here, the past gains meaning and serves as a foundation for interpreting the present. The responsibilities and risks of losing culture are attached to land and how we nurture and respect one another. ——

THE BROAD PICTURE

When I reached the village of Chi from Mon, this image |fig. 2| welcomed me. The Chief Minister of Nagaland and a host of officials had arrived, and the entire village lined up to welcome them. Women dressed in their traditional jewellery and men adorned themselves in warrior outfits for the event. The village Baptist church, the police escort jeeps that provide security to the VIPs and a welcome banner atop a bamboo gate cloaked in traditional Konyak attire established what is Naga culture today. We are simultaneously involved in official ceremonies, establishing power hierarchies and embracing Christianity and the English language as part of the Naga culture. Once I walked through the gate, I saw a large audience. ——

Fig. 2 Security personnel and Chi village residents at the entrance of the welcome gate erected to honour the Nagaland chief minister and VIPs

Fig. 3 Nagaland Chief Minister delivering a speech. Seated are the *Angh* (king) and the queens of Chi village with other state dignitaries

UNOFFICIAL ORDER OF CULTURE

There was a pathway that was cleared for the dancers to enter the stage and perform for the Chief Minister and the VIPs sitting on the podium |fig. 3|. Right in front of me were rows of children craning their neck to watch the event |fig. 1|. Unlike the elders, they were the only members who appeared *normal* and at home. Dressed in jackets, sweaters and pants that covered their bodies, they looked like they were at an event or visiting a cultural show. They were intelligent enough to know that this was just not how they lived life every day. I could see that they were curious and trying to understand the event unfolding in front of their eyes. Inspired by the gaze of children, I began to wonder what it means to explore Naga culture through the eyes of children. There was nothing normal about the culture on display at Chi. I was interested in capturing the expressions and gaze of these children as they engaged in the spectacle as members of the audience. ——

OFFICIAL ORDER OF CULTURE

The *Angh* (king) of the village of Chi with his two wives sat on the podium with the state officials. The Chief Minister of Nagaland gave a speech on Naga history and explained how the state of Nagaland loved the Konyak people. He unveiled a grand plan to build a Naga museum in Chi, in the Mon district, the *centre* of Naga culture. Seamlessly appointing himself as the head of the state, a benevolent friend and a Naga who represented the Naga people, he addressed the villagers of Chi as 'keepers of Naga culture'. A group of warriors dressed up in hornbill feathers carrying guns and *daos* (machetes) came in chanting and singing. Soon after they exited the stage, I followed them. Who were these warriors? Where did they come from? The image below reveals a moment where I witnessed what Naga culture calls it a day |fig. 4|. As the warriors changed back into their regular clothes to head back home, I realised how Naga culture exists in patches. Simultaneously worn with vests and shoes, with socks and track suits,

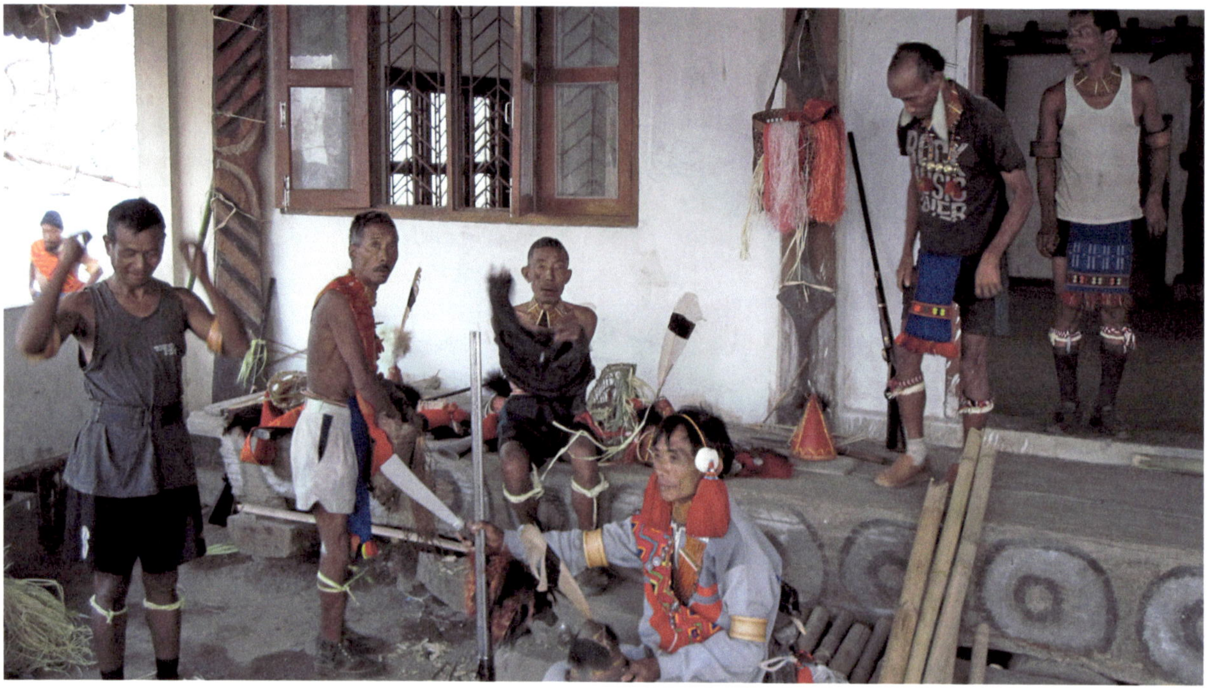

the Naga beads and headgears, the loin cloth and the guns, are all part of Naga culture. Everything is contained in the veranda of a concrete house with wooden beams that bear the totemic symbols of the tiger. Taken away from the podium and the official gaze, it is always the backstage where the freedom to imagine and engage with Naga culture begins.

IN SEARCH OF CULTURE

Much of my time in Mon was spent at the cultural show organised by the state of Nagaland. In 2010, the Mon Road Show was paired with the Aoleang festival, the annual harvest festival of the Konyak people. Like many people, I was also drawn to the local area. Here, I gathered with a host of tourists, visitors and a multitude of Konyak people who came to witness the show. Although the security guards requested the Konyak cultural troupes stay away from the podium, where the VIPs who were sitting and watching the show, the spirit of the place was vibrant. Inside the bamboo structures there were various stalls displaying arts and crafts. There were also government departments, like agriculture, rural development and industry that had set up shops to display governance and state initiatives in the Mon district.

Like me, there were visitors – researchers, photographers, journalists and tourists – although none of us identified ourselves as people aspiring to discover Naga culture. We were all busy examining, buying and consuming what was available in front of our eyes. While there were exciting events all around me, I ended up following a group of children who had come from a nearby village to witness the event. Amidst the cultural frenzy, the children appeared small and lost. Suddenly, they sat down and were immersed in watching a Konyak elder making a wooden sculpture of a Naga warrior. Although the people around them were focused on staffing the stalls displaying crafts like jewellery and textiles, this image captured my imagination with my own culture.

Dismantling the official narrative on Naga culture means adopting a decolonising framework to approach and reflect on Naga culture. How is Naga culture displayed? In what ways do we legitimise and adopt a Western gaze to situate Naga society? The younger generation of Nagas are discovering new ways of connecting with language and practices. However, land or community connections are undergoing great transformations as young people become migrants in search of livelihood options and economic opportunities.[2] The crowd, fascinated with Naga culture and in search of authentic experiences, made me examine the reality of market forces, employment questions and the reality of Indigenous culture as a site of entertainment. Many tourists at the event sought to get a close-up view of the dancers, eager to capture and experience a 'dying' cultural world. Such events that are staged to connect Naga culture and society fail to capture the profound transformation on the ground. What does it mean to *package* my living culture for global consumption in an amphitheatre for tourists and photographers?

For me, this experience allowed me to engage with the meanings of Naga society and culture. As a Naga anthropologist, the Mon district taught me how the state recognises Naga culture as a commodity to generate livelihoods and uphold market values. Extraction of coal, gender violence, child labour, prospects for hydrocarbon, tourism, migration and the rise of speculative plantation capital – these developments will connect the Naga children to their homelands in the future. And these realities will take place alongside tourists and travellers arriving in Nagaland on a quest to consume authentic culture with their cameras going *click, click, click*.

Fig. 4 Chi warrior dancers changing their outfit after the welcome event to honour the Nagaland Chief Minister, 2010

Fig. 5 Sash (*shukuju*), Ao Naga, Nagaland, latter half 19th century, hair, dye, cotton, wool, orchid stalks

Otto E. Ehlers Collection, donated in 1896 to the Royal Museum of Ethnology, Inv. No. IC28460, Staatliche Museen zu Berlin, Ethnologisches Museum

Fig. 6 Ear jewellery for men, Konyak Naga, Wancho (hist. Banpara, Joboka), Arunachal Pradesh, latter half 19th century, goat hair, rattan, orchid stalks

Samuel E. Peal Collection, donated in 1896 to the Royal Museum of Ethnology, Inv. No. IC28173f, Staatliche Museen zu Berlin, Ethnologisches Museum

1 Chishi 2012.

2 Kikon and Karlsson 2019.

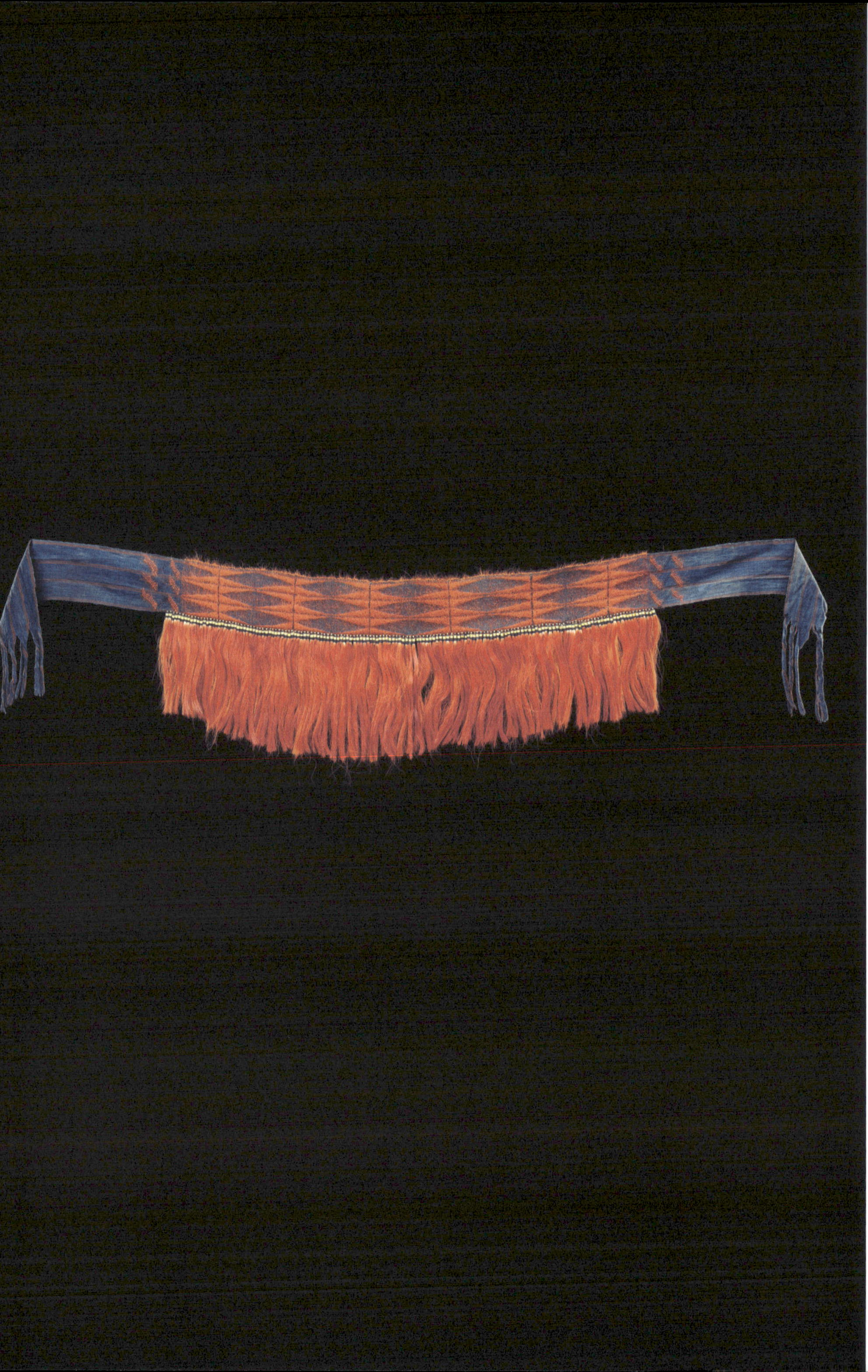

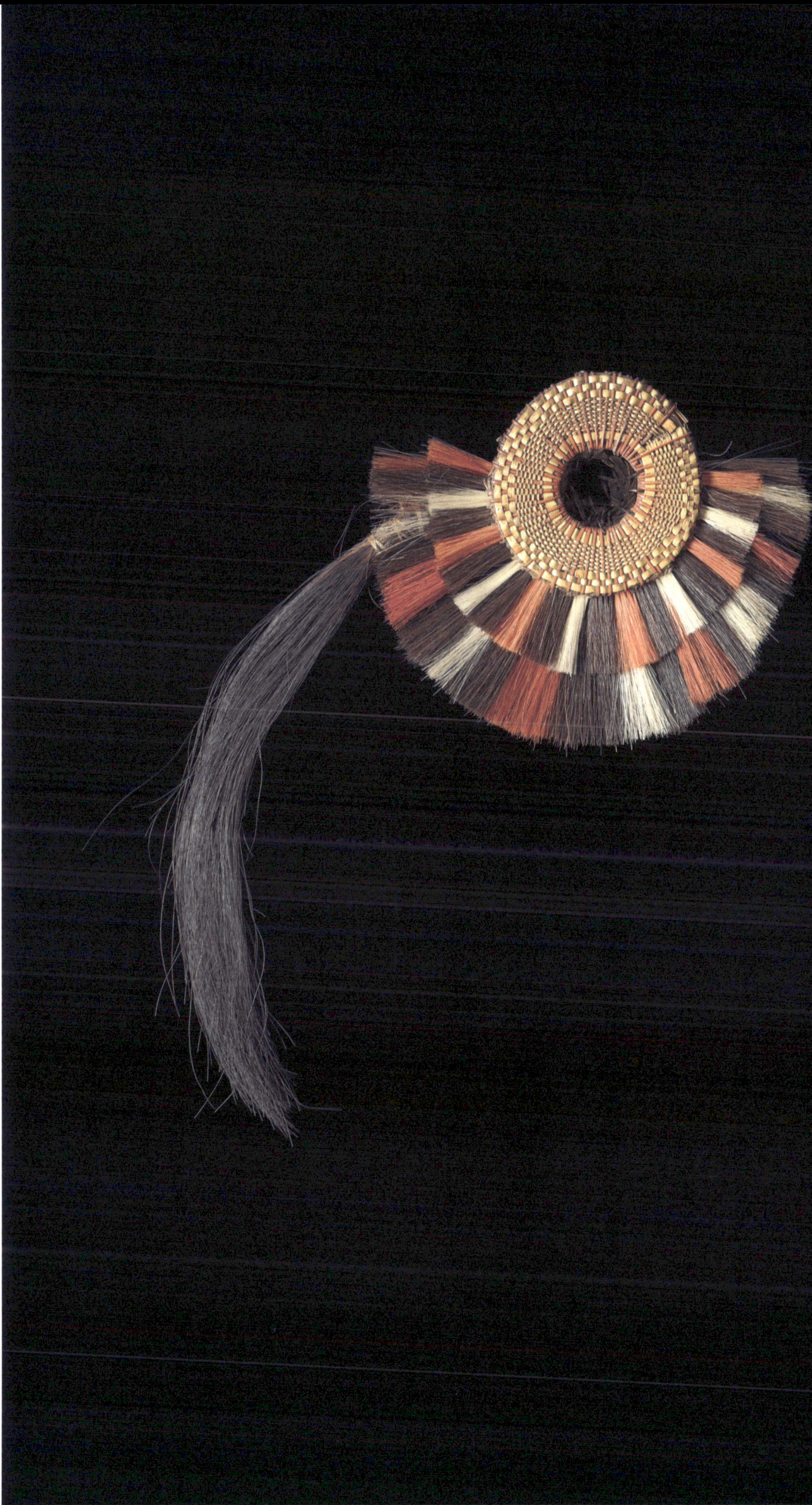

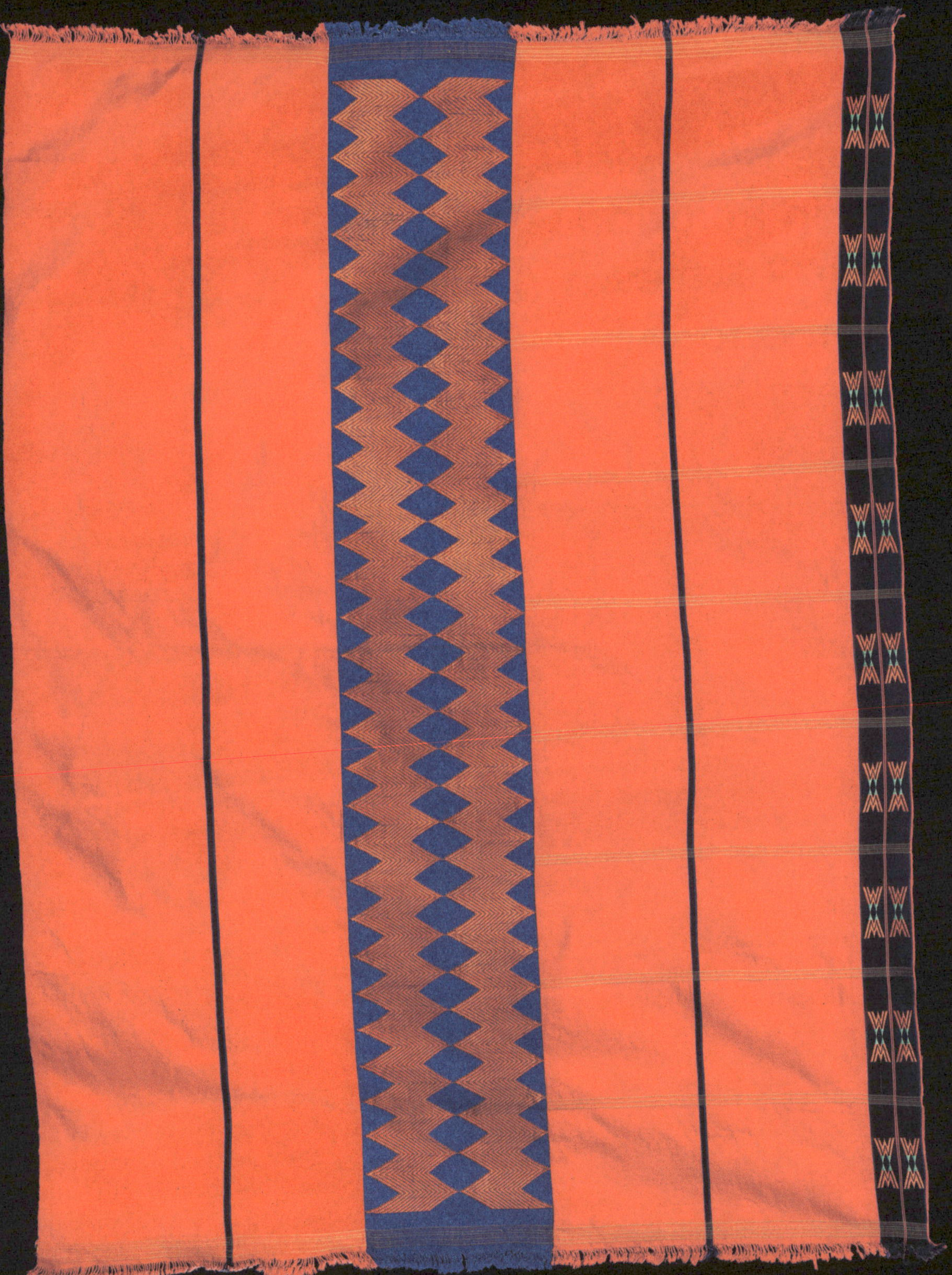

SOCIAL MEDIA, FASHION AND IDENTITY

The Role of Social Media in Relation to Naga Textiles, Fashion and the Creation of 'Naganess'

Theyiesinuo Keditsu

The body in traditional Naga culture is vocal and visible. If one can anachronistically conceptualise a Naga Self, it would be one that is embodied, one that is entrenched in networks of kinship. Whether it was gender, class, status within one's clan or village or one's broader village or tribal identity, it was the body first that declared it, before speech and pleasantries or conflict confirmed it. Beginning with markings and modification of the actual body, in the form of tattoos, piercings and hairstyles to clothing and adornments placed on the body, speaking with and through our bodies was a crucial and spectacular way of owning and conveying one's identity. It is no wonder then that fashion, in its modern sense, is a practice familiar to most Nagas.

Textiles are one of the key modes of articulating and expressing individual and collective identity in Naga culture. By reading the patterns created using certain combinations of colours and motifs, it is possible to place a textile as belonging to a tribe, or a group of villages in a geographical region (range) or a village, clan, gender, and learn about the wearer's family legacy or even his or her own personal achievements or circumstances. There are shawls and body clothes for men and women, there are some that can be worn by both – what in modern parlance we call unisex. Textiles commemorate achievements – in olden times, it would be heads taken, conquests in war, feasts of merit; in the present day, these same textiles are gifted to those who excel in their fields and bring renown and honour to their families, clans, village and tribes. Textiles confer status, textiles mark class – clothes for the rich and for the poor. Textiles mark celebration – cloths that can be worn for weddings, festivals or the coming of seasons – and they witness death and mourning. The sophisticated cacophony associated with the semiotics of contemporary fashion is not a modern (Western) invention. It is simply another corpus that fused readily onto a highly compatible syntax with which we were already highly proficient.

But there have been moments where this new corpus has threatened to eradicate our native vocabulary. First, in the moments of conversion to Christianity, when converts were exhorted or more often chastised to cover up – as if we were ever naked. The parts of our body we clothed failed to account for parts of our body we chose to leave uncovered. Puritanical notions of modesty and shame were inculcated through our indoctrination into Baptist Christianity. We began to view our bodies differently and see our clothes as inadequate in covering the literal and metaphorical nakedness of our indigenous bodies. So many took to wearing Western-style garments. The educated elite who could afford entirely Western outfits used their syntactical expertise in sartorial expression to dress themselves in the latest fashions. Lifestyles and behaviour of the elite percolate down social strata in the form of aspirations, and so those below them followed suit – Western dress, language and practices came to denote a civilised, modern identity. As we became more Christian and modern, the Naga body was the first battlefield to be compromised, but not conquered entirely. Textiles became a means for people

Fig. 1 Wrap skirt for women (*nongbu idset*), Chang Naga, Tuensang, Nagaland, 2018, handwoven synthetic fibre bought at the Tuensang Embroidery Center, Nagaland, in 2018 by the curators for the Stiftung Humboldt Forum in the Berlin Palace

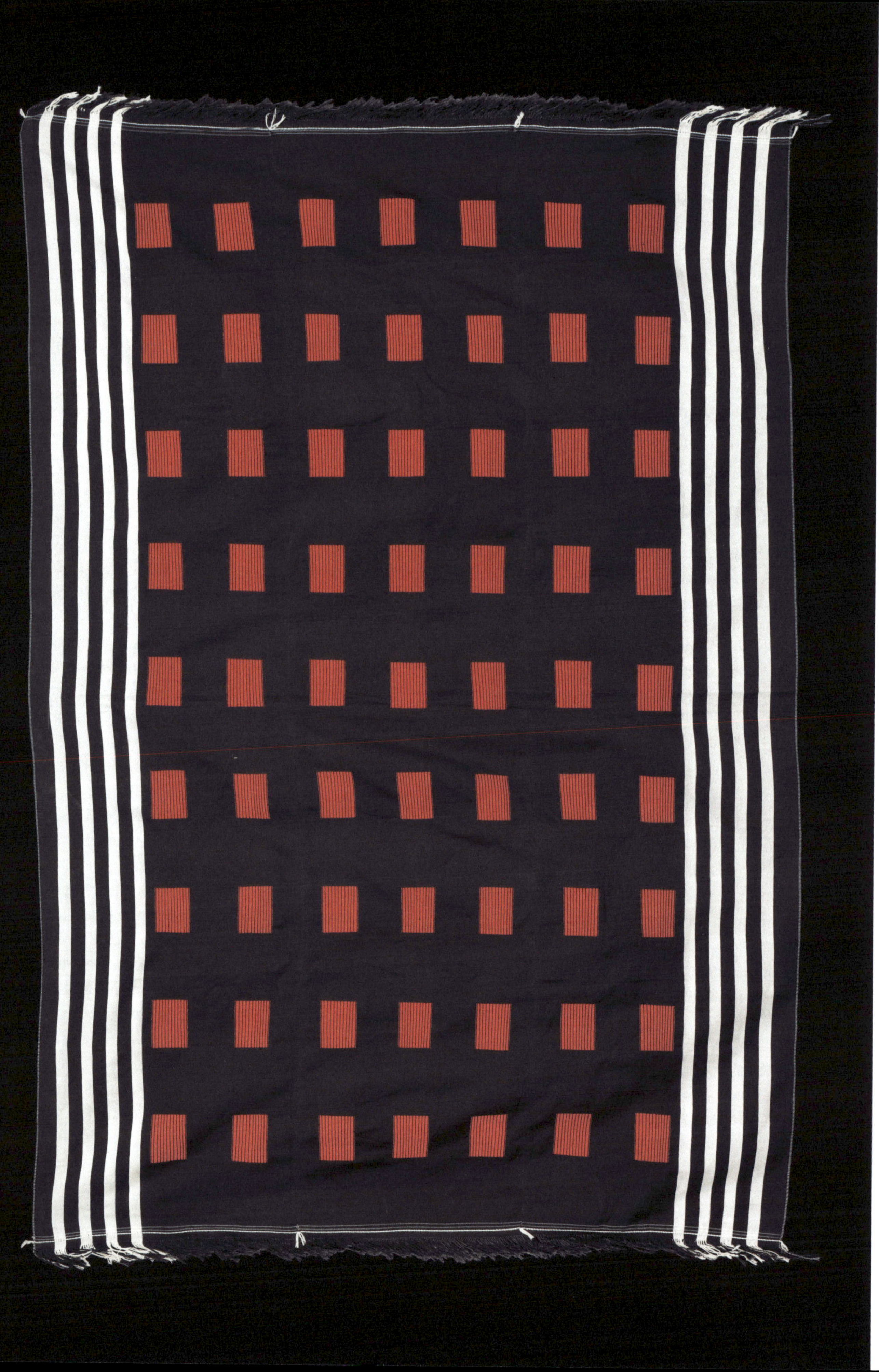

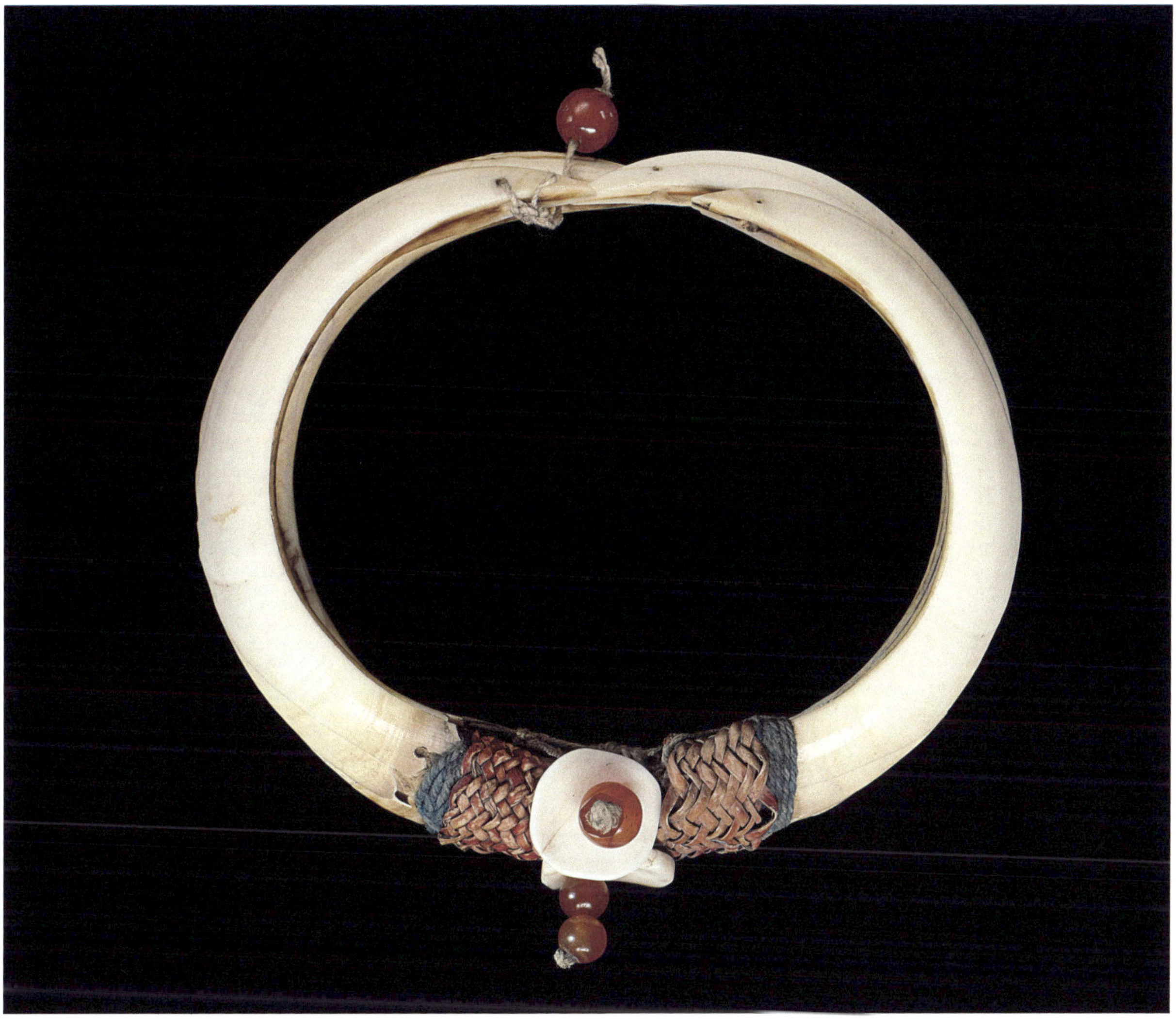

who were increasingly alienated from their indigenous way of life to hold on to some vestiges of a culture they were losing. If most of our traditional social institutions, practices, beliefs and material culture were rendered profane by Christianity or obsolete by modernity, then the use of textiles, albeit a gesture of tokenism, was one tether that kept us from becoming completely severed from our roots. Secondly, when India invaded Nagaland (or Naga lands), attire became a symbolic and non-violent way for Nagas to express our protest against the violence and atrocities unleashed on us. When the conflict stretched on and morphed into a more sophisticated hegemonic offensive, wearing Western and Naga attire became a way to resist the incursion of Indian culture. In the past two or three decades, however, Indian cultural industries have advanced and flourished, making deep inroads into Naga culture via mass and now social media as part of a larger, overwhelming wave of globalisation that has transformed the entire world. For some earlier generations, wearing Indian dress was sacrilegious and scandalous. Today, the *kurta*, in its ethnic and fusion forms, is a popular choice of dress for most Naga women as are the *salwar kameez*, *kurta pajama* and even *lehenga*.[1] The sari, however, still straddles the borders of censure and what is acceptable. —

In order to survey the role of social media in relation to textiles and fashion, we must first mark out the key moments where Naga textiles are visible. By Naga textiles, I mean textiles usually woven on the backstrap or loin loom with traditional motifs as well as contemporary ones. An acute crisis of identity is an almost universal corollary of globalisation, and one wave of responses has been the myr-

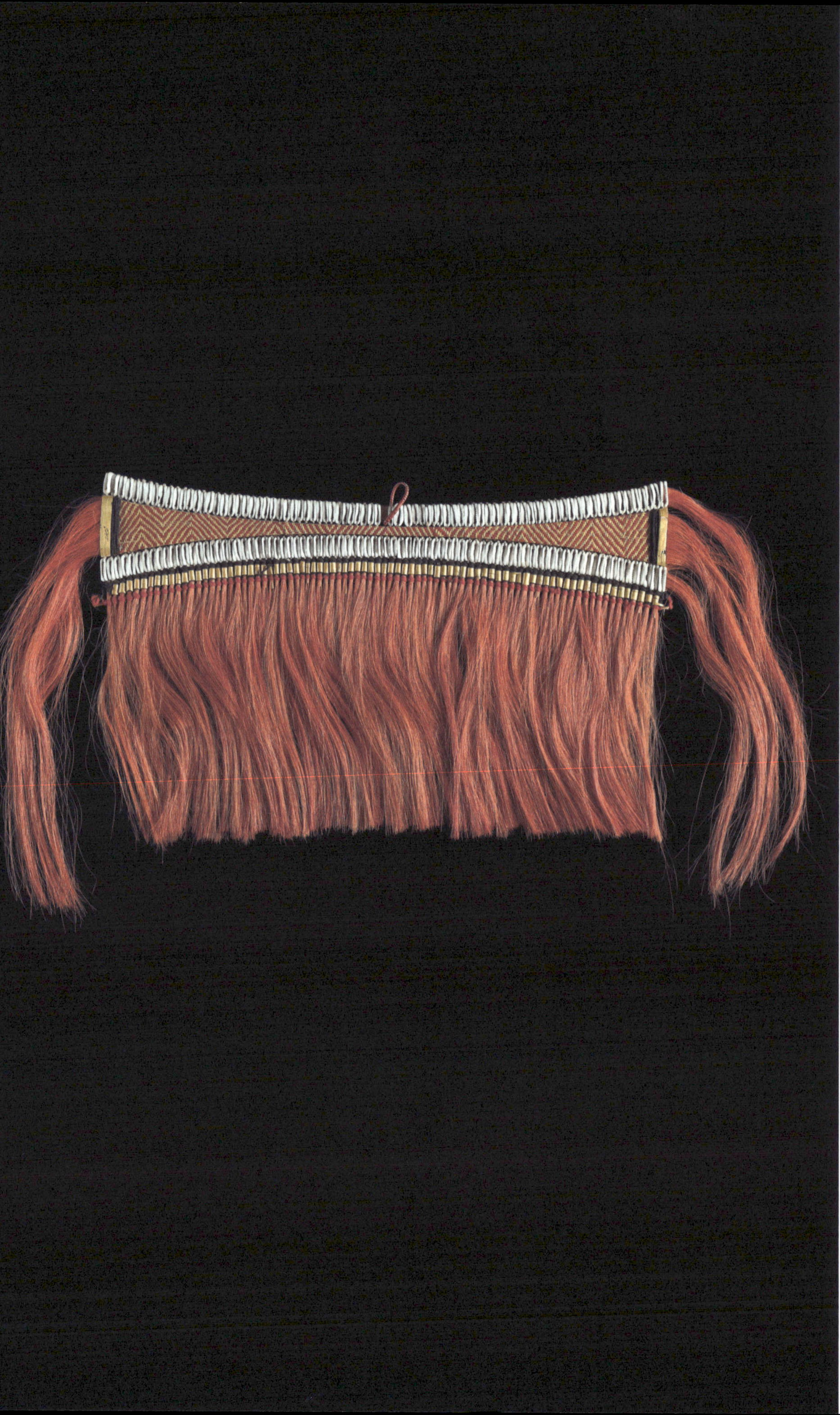

iad assertions and interventions that fall under the rubric of identity politics. For Nagas as a marginalised and oppressed minority forced into the Indian state, identity politics has become a predominant mode of redress as well as a means by which rights and justice can be pursued. Power dynamics among the over forty Naga tribes in Naga inhabited areas in India as well as Myanmar has meant that identity politics plays out in this domain as well. These developments provide a new context for textiles to emerge as a way of asserting identities that encompass 'Naganess' even as old modes of articulating one's regional, tribal, village, clan and individual identities are refracted through new media.

Fashion images involving Naga textiles can be divided into two categories. The first would be images that have been posted as a mode of recording or capturing outfits that have been worn 'IRL' – in real life. The past two decades have witnessed a resurgence in pride in our Naga identity. Nagas are beginning to contest the idea that Christianity entails separating ourselves from our traditional culture. Naga theologians, church leaders and congregants are beginning to explore modes of indigenising our Christian faith. In the process, wearing traditional textiles for Church services and functions have been on the rise. Where once choir uniforms were mostly Western-style clothes, uniforms and costumes created for performers – adult or child – are increasingly fusions of traditional textiles with Western wear or wholly traditional. In fact, significant Church events or moments such as commemorations of a tribe or village's conversion to Christianity are often marked by designing new textiles with symbolic and narrative meanings. Some churches have gone to the extent of explicitly encouraging their female members to wear *mekhalas* (clothes wrapped around the lower body and tucked in at the waist) giving rise to debates about how this imposition is another expression of patriarchal authority that perpetuates regressive notions of femininity. Most textiles are expensive and are usually not washed often due to the loss of lustre and tension, hence they are saved for special days – the most expensive ones usually for occasions like Christmas, Mother's or Father's Day, Easter and weddings.

Fig. 2 Shoulder cloth for men, Khiamnungan Naga, Noklak, Nagaland, 2018, synthetic fibre
bought in Noklak, Nagaland, in 2018 by the curators for the Stiftung Humboldt Forum in the Berlin Palace

Fig. 3 Neck jewellery (*tchipo*), Ao Naga, Nagaland, latter half 19th century, boar's tusks, carnelian, vegetable fibre, shells
Adolf Bastian Collection, sold in 1879 to the Royal Museum of Ethnology, Inv. No. IC8474, Staatliche Museen zu Berlin, Ethnologisches Museum

Fig. 4 Pectoral ornament (*keptang*), Ao Naga, Nagaland, latter half 19th century, hair, dye, cowrie shells, orchid stalks, woven vegetable fibre
Samuel E. Peal Collection, donated in 1896 to the Royal Museum of Ethnology, Inv. No. IC28461, Staatliche Museen zu Berlin, Ethnologisches Museum

Here, it is important to note the sexist, ageist and classist connotations at play in the use of textiles. The onus of wearing of textiles, whether regularly or on occasion, with all their implied political semiotics falling primarily on older women. Women of elite classes follow the traditional mode of wearing prestigious traditional textiles or expensive contemporary ones. Women of lower classes or from rural areas either wear traditional textiles that communicate their status or wear contemporary ones that are within their economic means. So, even on Christmas day, it is possible to look around and read the social standing of each woman based on the *mekhala* or shawl they are wearing. Until very recently, it was not common to see younger women wearing *mekhalas* or shawls to these occasions, unless they were wearing them as a uniform as participants. And among younger people, wearing traditional textiles still carries associations of backwardness – in mindset, class and society. Older men wear shawls and most men – old and young these days – wear waistcoats fashioned from shawls and motifs found in them.

Social media is primarily a space occupied by younger Nagas. For them, occasions such as annual cultural days in schools and colleges and the space of performance provided opportunities to dress 'up' in their traditional clothing. Fashion shows, which are a common and regular feature of fresher's day, farewells and social weeks in schools, colleges and universities, offer avenues for students to dress in traditional costume and to present contemporary fusion 'looks' that experiment with various permutations and combinations of our textiles, jewellery and accessories. Finally, popular artists such as the Tetseo Sisters, who are known as much for their music as their visually spectacular performance costumes, have set a trend among their contemporaneous performers to opt for traditional textiles rather than Western clothing. Images of textiles displayed on the bodies of Naga digital natives are mainly sourced from these occasions. Thus, these expressions of 'Naganess' are dramatic, spectacular and fall into the realm of the performative rather than reflecting any kind of embodied engagement with lived reality. ——————————

Nevertheless, these images have sprouted handles dedicated to featuring the costumes of specific tribes, regions or the Nagas in general. The popular Instagram account @nagastreetstyle with over 105,000 followers that, in their words, 'features stylish Nagas', has since 2017 included looks that incorporate Naga textiles. To the extent that now these traditional or fusion looks account for more than a third of their image output and are featured under the theme (and hashtag) #Roots. Handles like @nagastreetstyle operate by aggregating content generated by individual social media users in their personal handles. This circulation thus allows Nagas to explore their traditional identities via textiles in an imagined, creative and, yes, aspirational space. It becomes a way to simultaneously inhabit a lost indigeneity while navigating a modern landscape in real life, a dynamic that somehow transfers a feeling of being Naga from the space of the digital to the real person – as is evident in a hashtag #indigenouspride, which often accompanies these images; and to the extent that there is a growing tendency to create these looks or dress up with the ultimate intent of producing a photographic digital object. ——————————

This brings us to the second category of fashion images we encounter on social media: ones where models (male and female) have been deliberately styled in Naga textiles by professionals and photographed using current photographic and digital technology. These images depend upon and propagate nostalgia – for the costumes portrayed in these images are historically and culturally accurate while at the same time no longer existent in real life. These images become referents for users who wish to recreate traditional outfits and modes of dress. They are in that sense instructional and act as a kind of visual archive for knowledge about Naga ways of dress that we are losing as older generations pass. ——————————

My Instagram account @mekhalamama falls somewhere in between. I use this account to share information about traditional textiles I have collected through oral narratives. I also use this account to share personal anecdotal narratives about textiles that have been passed on to me by the women in my family and social circle. The looks I photograph are created both with the intent of turning them into a digital photographic object but are also outfits that I actually wear to work |see pp. 72–74|. While I am out and about in real life, the textiles on my body become secondary even inconsequential. And I am the first one to do this on social media. A consequence of my experiments has been that many Naga women (and to a lesser degree men) have re-examined their notions of textiles as unsuited for everyday life, as costume. In the years since 2017, when I started my account, it is more common to see young women wearing *mekhalas* to church and to other formal occasions – many of them as part of a commitment they have made to join the #mekhalamovement I started on social media. It is important to note that most of these women, young and old, belong to the urban, educated demographic. Most rural women don't have the luxury to choose what they want to wear. For that matter, when we talk about social media use in the context of Nagaland, we must note that this is a facility and world not accessible to many, and particularly those in rural areas where either there is poor internet or cell phone coverage or people cannot afford smartphones. What my account has done is reorient their attitude towards the textiles they wear from one of resignation to agency. ——————————

The increasing visibility of textiles on social media is simultaneously a result of their growing fashion value and feeds back into impetuses that make them more 'cool' and in demand. This current trend percolates down social strata in the form of aspirational value as well as real income for weavers generally belonging to lower-income or rural households. In the process, Nagas are able to incorporate their textiles into looks that express their identities as Nagas and citizens on par with their counterparts in the digital arena and real world. By expressing and enabling a resurgence in #indigenouspride, textiles on social media empower creators and consumers of the fashion images. In real life, they also empower women who weave and ensure the survival of a threatened art form. ———

1 *Salwar kameez* is a women's dress consisting of a long blouse, pants and shawl. *Kurta* is a long men's 'blouse', *lehenga* is a long women's dress similar to the sari.

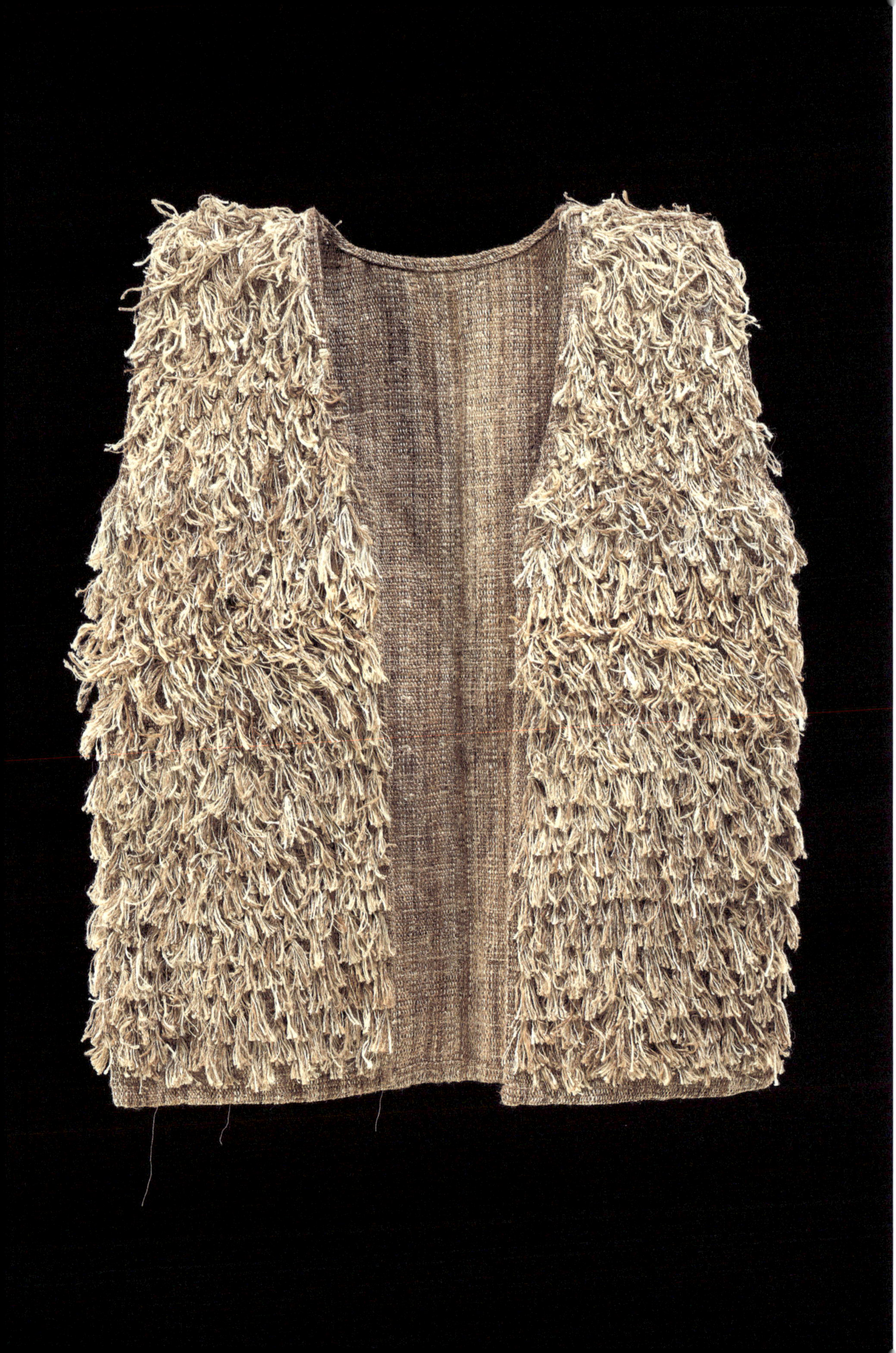

NAGA TEXTILES Living Tradition Exemplified

Elisabeth Seyerl-Langkamp

Starting with the collection of historic Naga artefacts, at the Berlin Ethnological Museum, *Naga Land: Voices from North-east India* is an exhibition that provides insights into Naga society today and to do so addresses the following relevant questions: What does being a Naga really mean? How does tradition, however defined,[1] influence the Naga of today? And what significance is associated with these historic objects from the Berlin collection in the processes of creating identity?[2]

Zubeni Lotha, co-curator of the exhibition, who is from Nagaland, has the following answer to this last, urgent question: 'Objects made by the Naga may be in a museum yet they still play an important role in the present. They are not dead objects at all. Perhaps they have lost their original significance and original functions; however, they are still being lived, reinterpreted and used in the widest-ranging ways imaginable.'[3]

In the above statement Lotha is referring to the Naga collection at the Berlin Ethnological Museum as a whole. The following text, on the other hand, is concerned with a specific group of objects within the collection: textiles. They play a major role in the present exhibition because (handwoven) fabrics are an aspect of Naga culture that has survived up to the present, despite colonialism and Christianisation and the societal changes that came with these two. Most importantly, textiles are, as Zubeni describes them, 'being lived', meaning they are still being made (by hand), featuring new designs or uses, and worn (everyday as well).

Fig. 1 Jacket made of nettle fibres, woven by Tokpan from the village of Noklak

NAGA TEXTILES PAST AND PRESENT

Shoulder-cloths, scarves and wrap-around skirts represent the most important traditional articles of Naga clothing, but for some years now they have been supplemented by new forms of clothing such as men's jackets.[4] The range of textile designs attributed to specific Naga groups is quite broad. In the past the attribution to one specific group seems to have been less stringent than now.[5] Historic fabrics, woven on backstrap looms (loin looms), incorporated unusual organic materials, such as orchid stems and dyed dog hairs.[6] Now mainly synthetic yarns and plastic appliqués are used for the same purposes to be woven into fabrics. How and when fabrics were to be worn was unambiguously regulated in the past. Clothes, jewellery and tattoos expressed membership of a specific social group as well as gender and social status. Simple fabrics were worn every day. On the other hand, for special occasions, such as a feast of merit organised by families for the whole village to enhance their own social status, special clothing was flaunted.

The first contact with the British in the early nineteenth century ushered in radical changes in Naga clothing. Indigenous cultural practices were forbidden, and with the ban on local religion and rituals imposed by Baptist missionaries, the textiles specifically associated with them also lost their significance. Nor were pupils attending Baptist schools permitted to wear Naga dress, and as a consequence Western dress had become widespread among educated Naga by the 1920s. The years of armed conflict with India after the country had achieved independence from colonial rule also led to the destruction of old textiles because numerous Naga villages were burnt down.

Although Western clothing figures predominantly in the look favoured by most Naga nowadays,[7] change has taken place in recent years, and preserving the ancient textile tradition is now promoted by local governments and the church as well as by smaller NGOs.[8] The ongoing trend can justifiably be

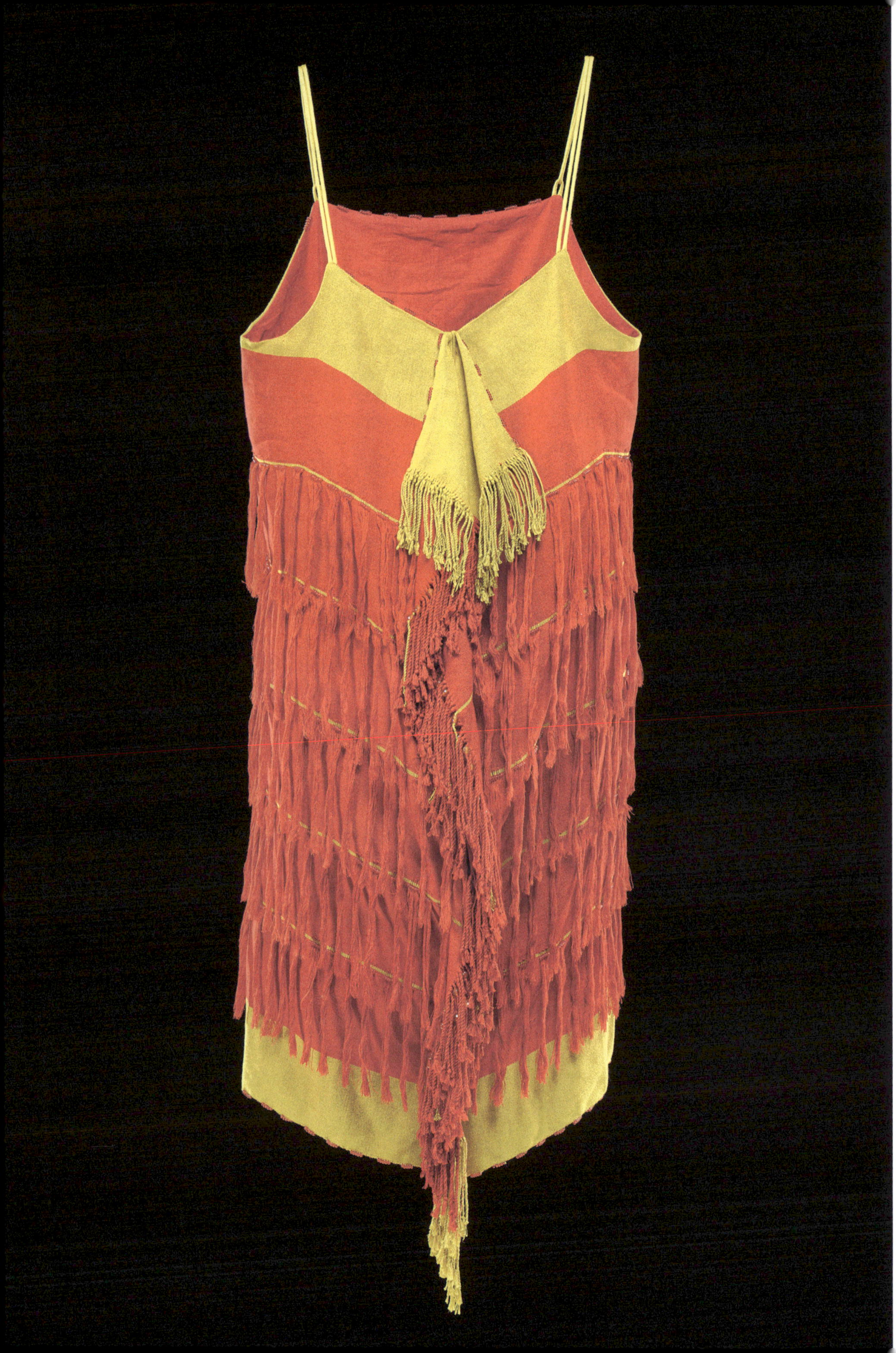

interpreted as a revival of traditional textiles. Naga fabrics are mainly worn for formal or special occasions such as church attendance, festive ceremonies[9] or cultural festivals. They are also encountered in local fashion design. Revisiting the venerable Naga textile tradition has in part to do with the search for a Naga identity that is demarcated from the rest of India. Some of those concerned also define being Naga by using the term 'Naganess'.[10] The emphasis is on an overarching Naga identity that unites the different Naga groups.

EXAMPLES OF OBJECTS

The selection of exhibits for this show is intended to place particular emphasis on common ground between past and present, continuity or breaks with tradition as exemplified by the historic textiles in Berlin and the fabrics produced and worn in Nagaland today. In addition, a wide range of designs and materials will be shown. About half of the textiles shown are 'traditional' (as viewed from today's standpoint) cloths worn by men and women in the nineteenth and early twentieth centuries. Drawn from a variety of Naga groups, they are shown together with jewellery to provide insights into Naga customs of dress and adornment in earlier days.[11] The historic textiles from the collection have been supplemented by new acquisitions. Most of these new objects were bought during a research trip to Nagaland in late 2018. In making their selection of objects, the curators[12] always had the historic pieces in Berlin in mind. The objects assembled were to demonstrate that Naga textile traditions are still very much alive, also in the form of fashion design. As each object was acquired, the name of the weaver or designer was documented because important information of this kind is lacking for the historic pieces – in addition brief interviews supplement some of the new objects shown in the exhibition.

Fig. 2 Imcha Imchen had a new version of his Tassel Dress woven especially for the exhibition. This is the back of the dress.

Fig. 3–5 Theyie Keditsu posts her outfit almost every day on Instagram.

NETTLE FIBRES

Tokpan is a weaver who lives in the village of Noklak. While working on an unusual textile, a jacket made of nettle fibres (fig. 1), she explained that weaving fabric out of this material rarely occurs nowadays because nettle fibres are very expensive and difficult to process. Tokpan in fact only uses nettle yarns for work on commission, for instance for Iris Odyuo, an ethnologist and artist[13] who accompanied the curatorial team as a guide and translator in Nagaland. Iris uses the materials as canvas to paint on and in so doing supports the preservation of this form of weaving.

MINISKIRT

The Tuensang Embroidery Center in the town of Tuensang markets a wide range of traditional articles of clothing and accessories. Along with a man's jacket, cloths and jewellery, a girl's miniskirt featured in the exhibition was acquired in the Tuensang Embroidery Center. The stylish garment is black and boasts a blue woven pattern of metallic threads. Cut very differently from the usual Nagaland women's wrap-around skirts, the miniskirt attests to the fact that the Naga textile tradition is being inspired by Western fashions in response to prevailing fashion tastes among the young generation.

TASSEL DRESS

Some years ago beauty contests incorporating fashion shows financed by local government laid the cornerstone for modern fashion design in Nagaland.[14] Imcha Imchen, a Naga fashion designer, repeatedly channelled the Naga textile tradition, particularly in his early designs, such as the Tassel Dress (fig. 2). Imchen drew his inspiration for it from a classic Ao Naga women's scarf.[15] A few years ago his Tassel Dress was worn by the Tetseo Sisters, a popular folk band in Nagaland, as their stage outfit. The band incorporates elements from various Naga groups in their music; this is their way of celebrating an overarching Naga identity. For the exhibition, Imcha had the dress,

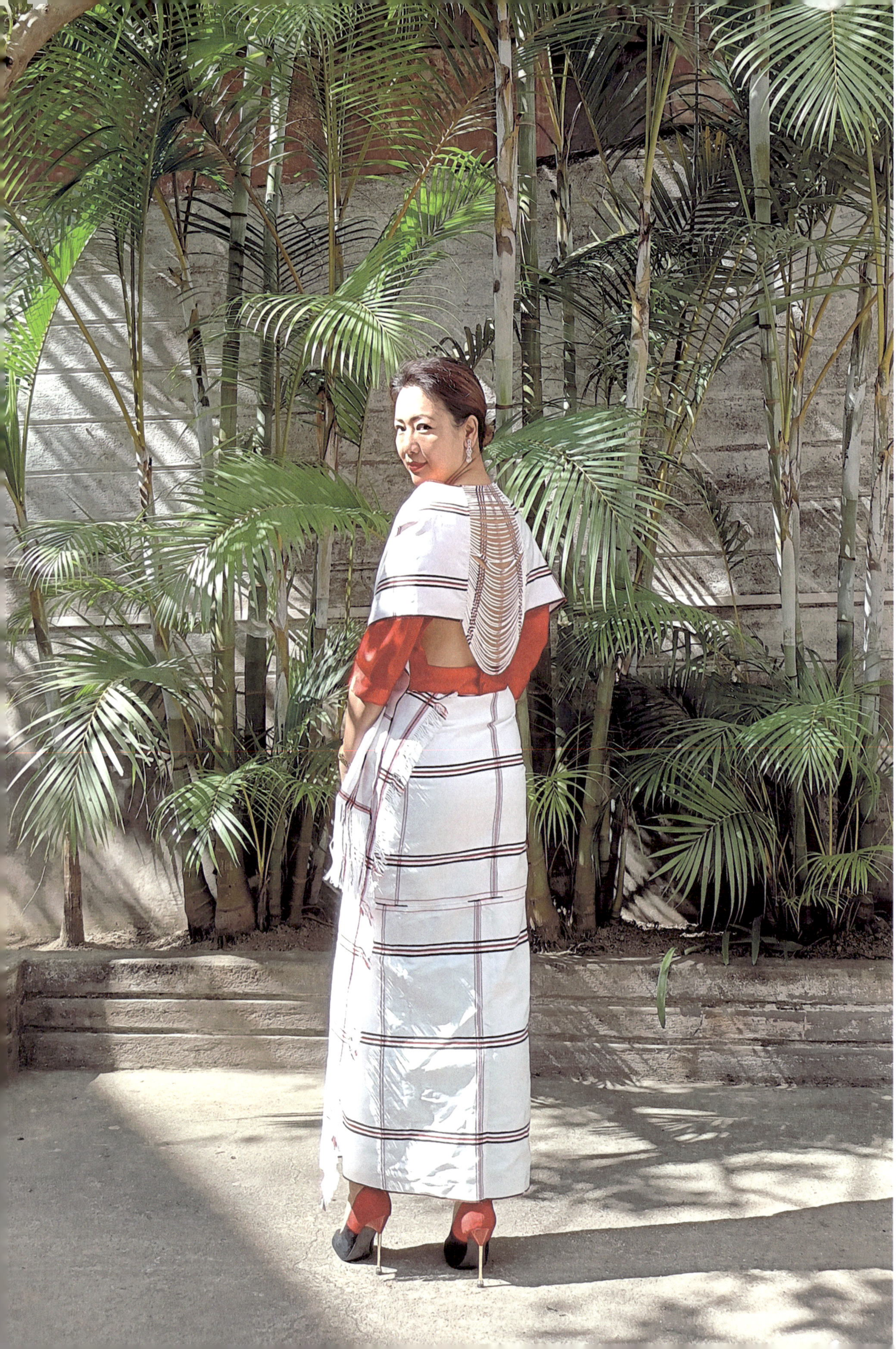

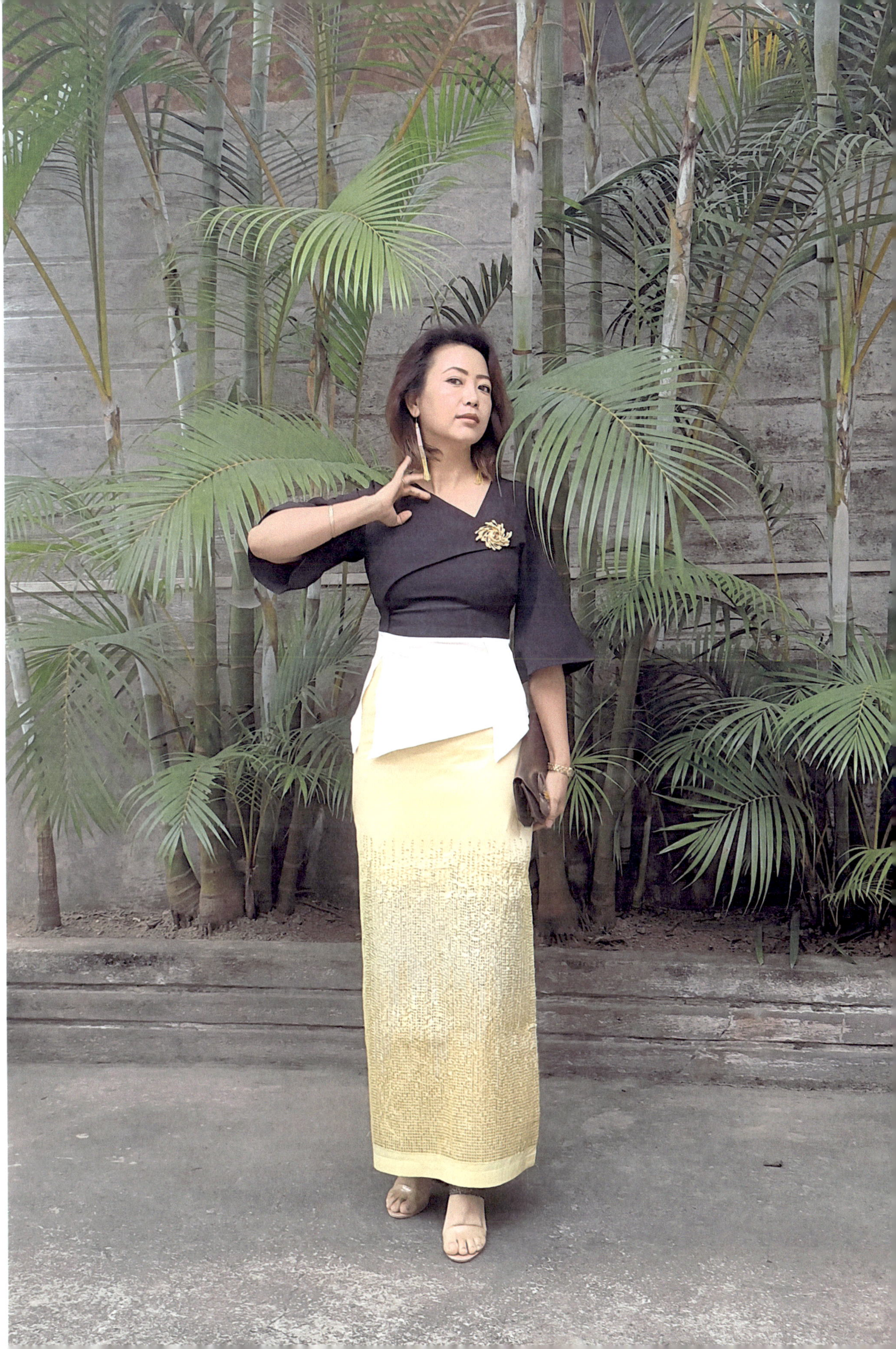

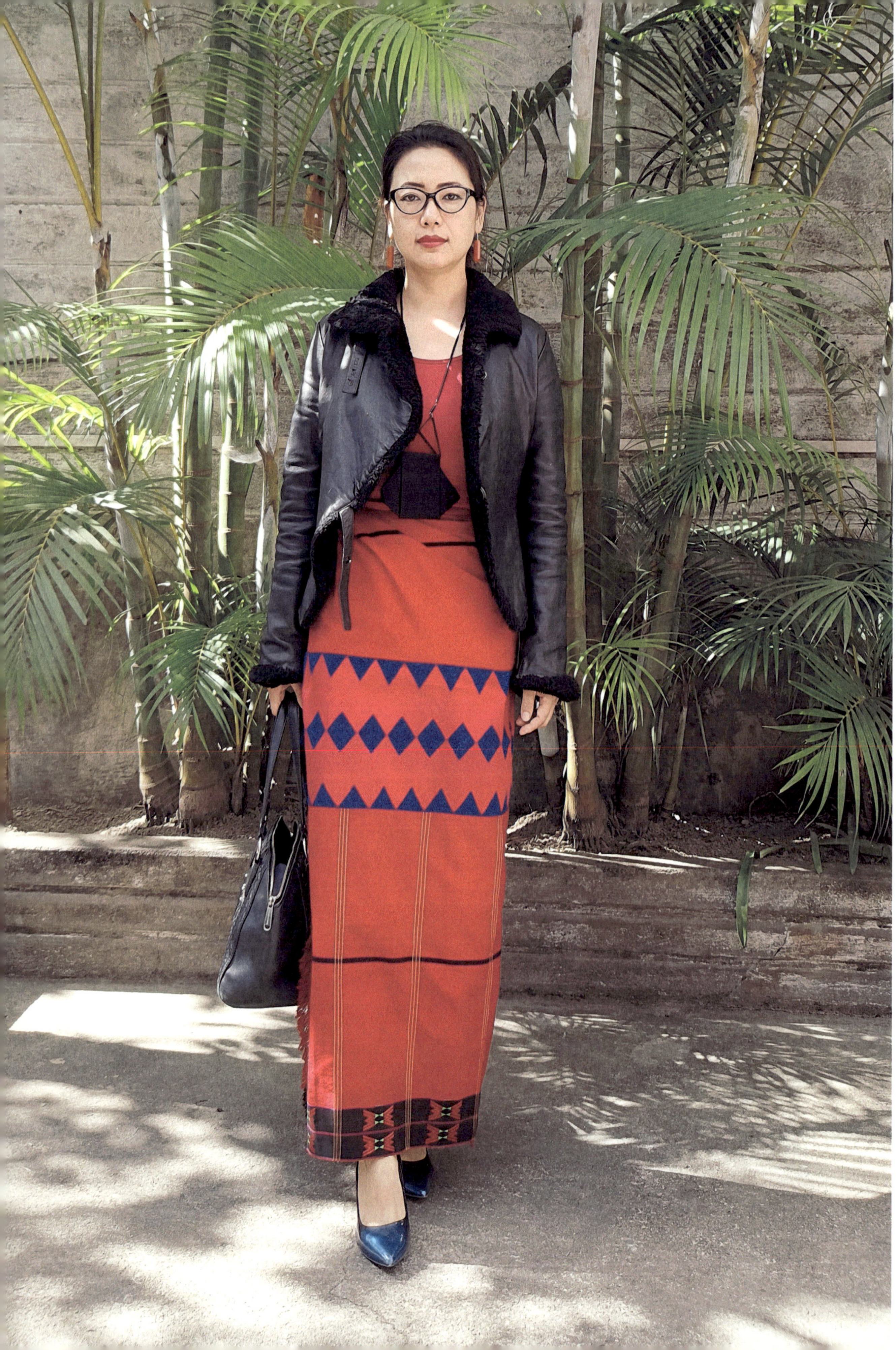

which was originally designed in black and white, woven in different colours.

A SHORT ONLINE SEARCH …

Reveals how younger Naga are approaching their textile tradition nowadays. The online activities of two Naga women in fashion are shown in the exhibition. First, there is Theyie Keditsu,[16] who is very successful with her Instagram account @mekhalamama (figs. 3–5). She almost daily posts a shot of herself, dressed in a *mekhala*, a women's wrap skirt. Her aim is to free this article of clothing from the prejudices attached to it and establish it as a modern business outfit for women of all ages: 'They associated draping *mekhalas* with women who were older, from rural areas or the working class. Many perceived it as an uncomfortable garment, which is ironic considering that less than 25 years ago, most Naga women wore only *mekhalas*. Instagram allows me to confront many of these biases and lets me explore the many possible reasons for why we think about our traditional dresses in the way we do.'[17]

Another interesting example of how Naga textiles are being reinterpreted is the work of the young stylist Asenla Jamir.[18] She is currently selling vintage clothing upcycled with Naga fabrics,[19] thus following the international trend towards second-hand fashion and upcycling. In the exhibition she is represented with a fashion photograph (fig. 6). In the photo, a girl is wearing jogging trousers and a T-shirt with Naga jewellery. This type of jewellery is today not only worn for cultural festivals or events put on for tourists but is also sold at hip boutiques like *Runway Nagaland* in Dimapur, the capital of Nagaland. The shop sells fashion 'Made in Nagaland'.[20]

Quite a large range of textiles and styles, ranging from classic handloom fabrics acquired from Naga villages to upcycled vintage fashion items, can be subsumed under the term 'Naga textile tradition'. As it did in the past, presenting one's clothing, be it at church, the Hornbill Festival or on social media, plays an important role. The makers, wearers and promoters of Naga textiles are, however, also concerned with preserving a tradition they look back on with pride. As far as textile design is concerned, there is a strong continuity, even though the rules governing the use of specific patterns or clothing designs have in many cases lost their meaning and a certain degree of standardisation has taken place. Materials and colours, too, have changed, and in many cases the quality of the modern textiles cannot be compared to the historic objects. Most importantly, textiles are used to express a certain identity, either promoted by the government or done out of personal interest.

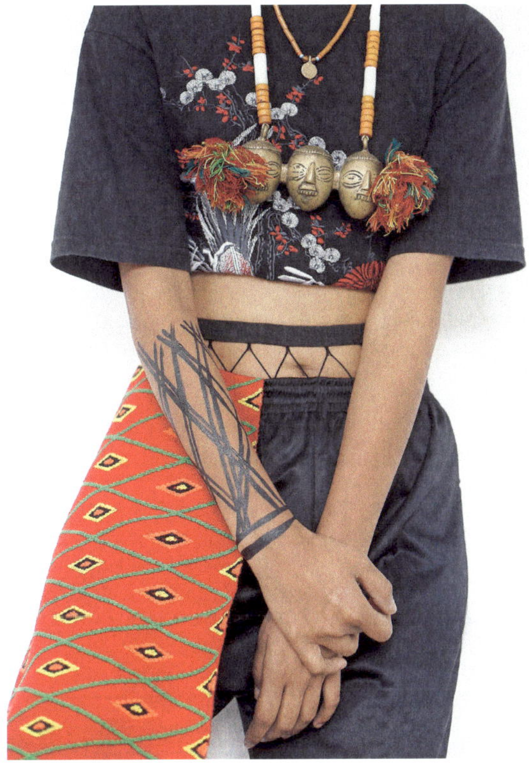

Fig. 6 Asenla Jamir's styling for her graduate diploma project combines Western fashion with Naga jewellery and textiles.

1 The term 'tradition' or 'traditional textiles' is quite problematic because it is often understood to describe something static, unlike 'fashion', which is understood to be innovative and new. When subjected to closer scrutiny, however, it often becomes clear that so-called traditional textiles and clothing were also informed by innovation and change and, most importantly, still are. Drawing on historic textiles in the Pitt Rivers Museum in Oxford, Vibha Joshi has confirmed this is true of Naga textiles. Unfortunately, however, it is difficult to eschew the term 'traditional' entirely. John Picton has suggested the term 'textile tradition' as an alternative to the phrasing 'traditional textiles'. See Joshi 2000, p. 382.

2 A database exchange project planned by Roland Platz and the Ethnological Museum in Berlin will study the significance of the historic Berlin Naga collection.

3 See https://www.preussischer-kulturbesitz.de/newsroom/dossiers-und-nachrichten/dossiers/dossier-magazin-internationale-kooperationen/auf-der-suche-nach-identitaet-die-naga-ausstellung-im-humboldt-forum.html (accessed 20 July 2022).

4 A brief note on the sources as they stand: Marion Wettstein and Vibha Joshi have written most of the specialist literature on Naga textiles. Online magazines and social media are especially important sources for fashion.

5 Wettstein points out that earlier ethnologists conveyed the impression that specific Naga groups were recognisable from their clothing. The boundaries, however, seem to have been more fluid: fabrics were probably used by several Naga groups. Nowadays, on the other hand, a strong standardisation is noticeable in designs. If you look at events organised for tourists, such as the Hornbill Festival that takes place annually in Nagaland, you get the impression each Naga group has specific textile designs. See Wettstein 2014, p. 195.

6 A study of fibres of an Ao Naga women's cloth (I C 28378 b) initiated by Kerstin Flemming, conservator at the Ethnological Museum in Berlin, revealed that dog hairs had been woven into the fabric.

7 Privately owned Naga photographs from the latter half of the twentieth century are shown in the exhibition. Most of the people in the photographs are wearing Western fashions.

8 An example to be cited in the present connection is the International Loinloom Festival, organised by Exotic Echo, a non-governmental organisation (NGO): see www.exoticecho.org.

9 Wettstein compares the fashion shows put on today, which are organised and sponsored by local governments, with the former feasts of merit. See Wettstein 2013, p. 77.

10 The term 'Naganess' is repeatedly used although the origins and meaning are not quite clear. According to Iris Odyuo, 'Naganess' means feeling comfortable with one's own culture. A member of the Tetseo Sisters band has chosen 'Naganess' as the title for her blog: www.naganess.com. As she defines it, the term is made up of the words 'Naga' and 'princess'.

11 In the exhibition historic photographs taken by Otto E. Ehlers from the Ethnological Museum in Berlin supplement the objects shown. Some of the textiles in the photographs are identical with artefacts in the museum collection.

12 The persons referred to are Roland Platz and the author representing the curatorial team.

13 See the essay by Iris Odyuo in this publication.

14 As a region, Northeast India is described as fashion conscious on the whole. Wettstein also views this claim as strategy deployed by the Indian government to lend the Northeast a new image: fashion and glamour rather than conflict and struggles for independence. See Wettstein 2013, p. 73, 84. Also see https://www.idiva.com/fashion/trends/why-north-easterners-always-have-the-best-sense-of-style/18004402.

15 See Ao Naga women's scarf (I C 28378 b), Ethnological Museum Berlin.

16 See the essay by Theyie Keditsu in this publication.

17 See https://www.verve-magazine.in/people/championing-the-sartorial-value-of-traditional-textiles-the-yiesinuo-keditsu (accessed 20 July 2022).

18 See https://rootsandleisure.com/asenla-jamir-fashion-stylist-singer-actor-assam/ (accessed 20 July 2022).

19 Second-hand fashion played an important role in Nagaland even before the Corona crisis, i.e., not just since about 2020, but the younger generation has developed stronger awareness of vintage clothing since the pandemic. See https://www.instagram.com/otsuclothingco/; https://www.voguebusiness.com/sustainability/how-covid-19-encouraged-india-to-shop-secondhand (accessed 20 July 2022).

20 See https://www.runway-india.in/collections/gtj-premium-collections (accessed 20 July 2022).

Fig. 7 Ear jewellery for men (*theher nyie*), Angami Naga, Nagaland, latter half 19th century, goat hair, dye, Job's tears (*Coix lacryma-jobi*), insect wings

Otto E. Ehlers Collection, donated in 1896 to the Royal Museum of Ethnology, Inv. No. IC26291, h–i, Staatliche Museen zu Berlin, Ethnologisches Museum

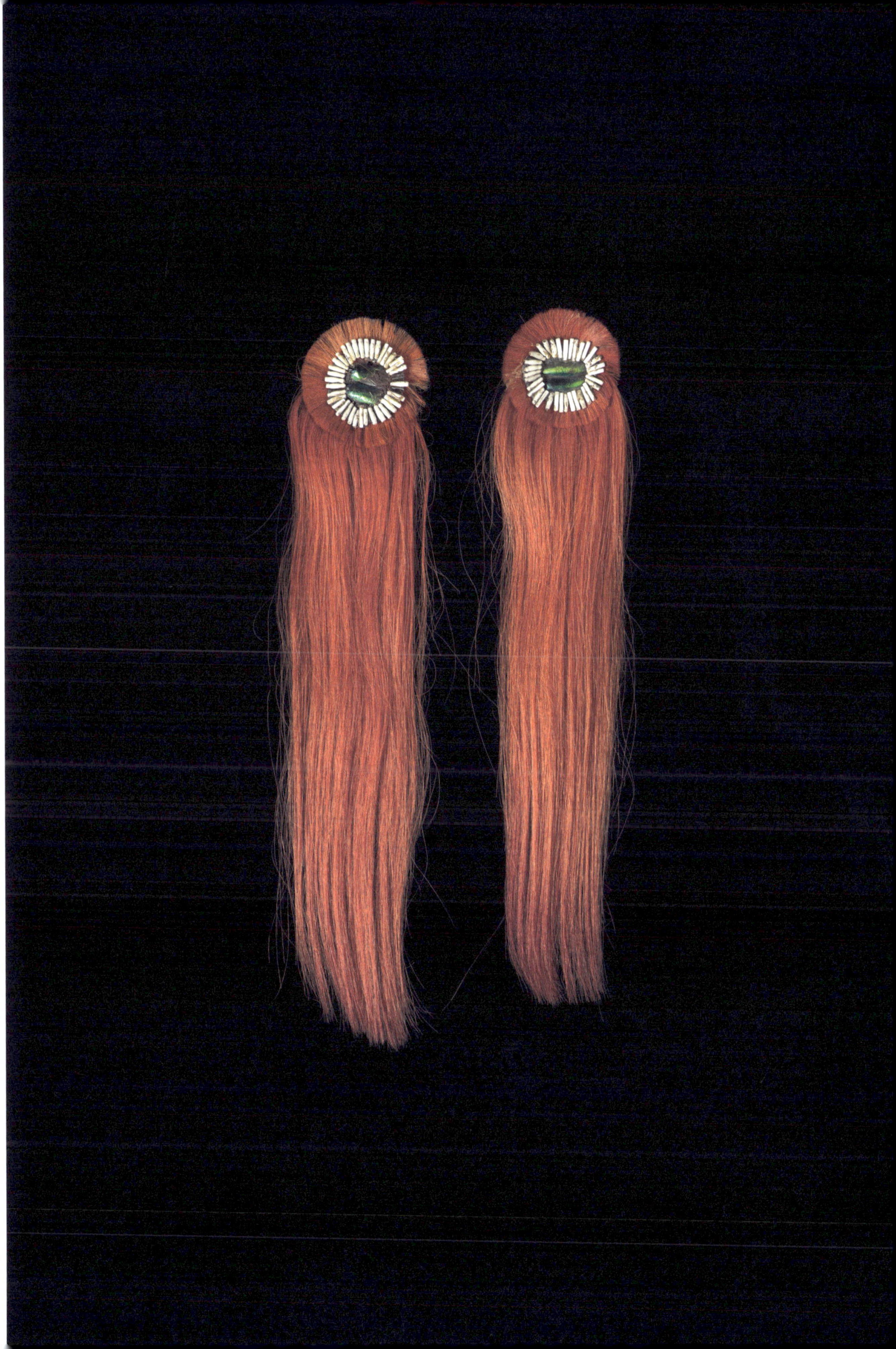

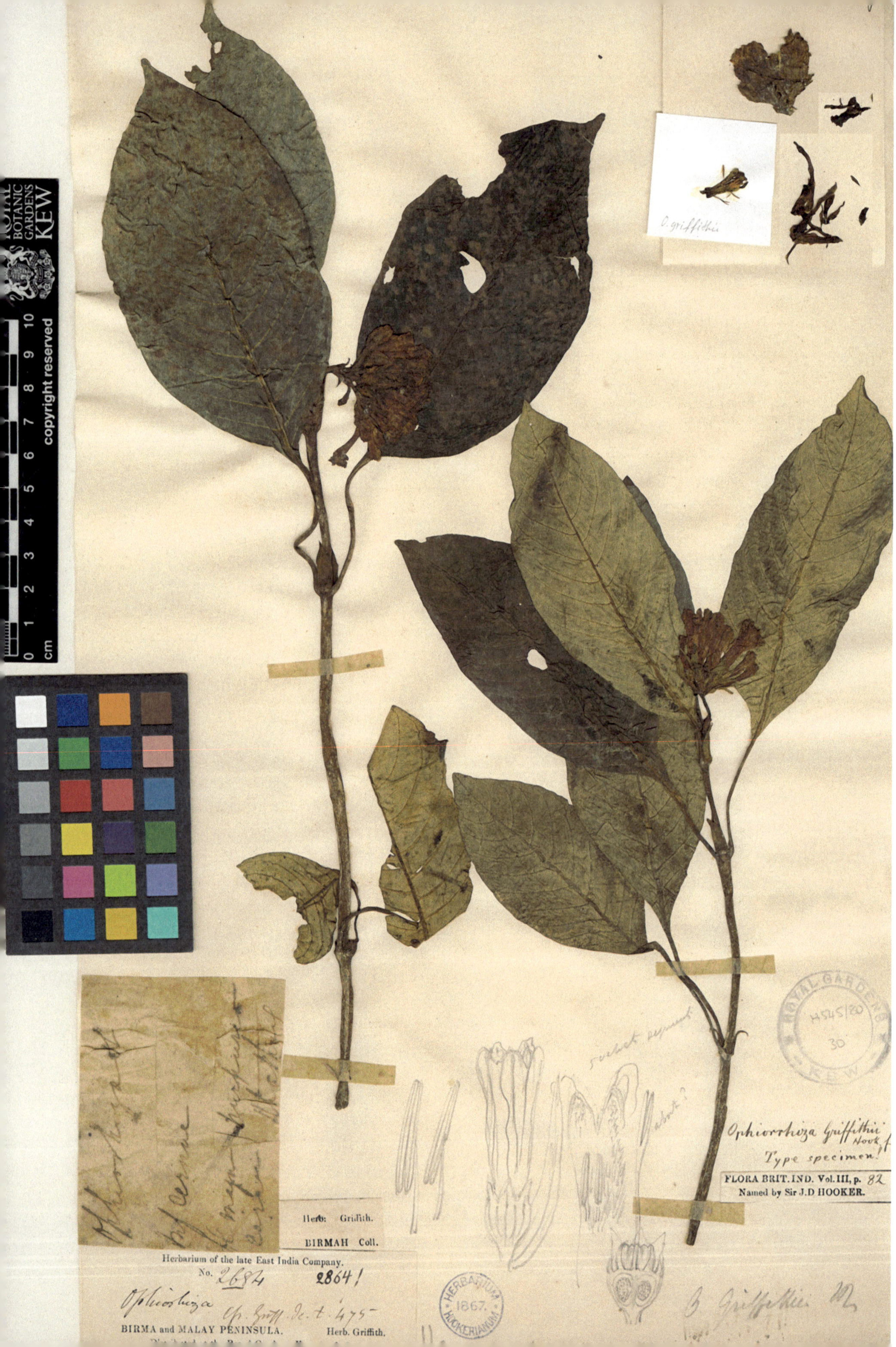
ROYAL BOTANIC GARDENS KEW
copyright reserved
cm 0 1 2 3 4 5 6 7 8 9 10
O. griffithii
Ophiorrhiza Griffithii Hook. f.
Type specimen!
FLORA BRIT. IND. Vol. III, p. 82
Named by Sir J.D HOOKER.
ROYAL GARDENS KEW
Herb: Griffith.
BIRMAH Coll.
Herbarium of the late East India Company.
No. 2684
28641
BIRMA and MALAY PENINSULA.
Herb. Griffith.
HERBARIUM 1867 HOOKERIANUM

HUNTING FOR TEA AND RUBBER
The Beginnings of Botanical Exploration in the Naga Hills

Kathrin Grotz

The history of early botanical exploration in the Naga Hills and the neighbouring mountainous regions is unthinkable without the expansion of the British Empire and its thirst for raw plant materials. In western Europe, botany was viewed in the nineteenth century as an exclusive pastime to be engaged in by the social elites. Practitioners of botany – the overwhelming majority of them men – aimed at nothing less than discovery, description and systematic classification of all plants worldwide. The universalist ambition driving the *scientia amabilis* lost its innocence at the latest when scientific and economic interests began to overlap in colonial contexts. Botanical field research also began in this way in the north-east of what is now India, as targeted bio-prospecting, i.e., expeditions organised for the purpose of systematically ascertaining the commercial potential of plant resources, supported by the Botanic Gardens in Calcutta (Kolkata) and Kew in London that were provided with a military escort for protection.

Fig. 1 The plant on this herbarium sample was collected in the Naga Hills by William Griffith in 1837. This is attested by the pencil inscription on the lower edge of the sample. The sheet took a roundabout route to reach Joseph Dalton Hooker, director of Kew Gardens, London. As the label attached to the right-hand corner indicates, Hooker described the plant in his botanical work, The Flora of British India, as new to science and gave it the name *Ophiorrhiza griffithii*. His choice of species name honours the late collector William Griffith – a taxonomic practice that is still widespread in botanical circles.

After the British East India Company had annexed Assam in 1826 from the Bamar people, steam ships began to ply the fertile valley of the Brahmaputra, bringing a steady stream of soldiers and settlers to the newly acquired province in north-eastern British India. The mountainous regions around the Assam floodplain, including what is now the Indian state of Nagaland, remained virtually unexplored for decades. Expeditions did sporadically advance as far as these regions because the British East India Company was desperately looking for land suitable for tea plantations to break the Chinese monopoly on tea growing, processing and marketing and to meet growing demands for the luxury beverage from all classes of English society with products of its own.[1]

To that end, Lord William Bentinck, who was appointed governor general of British India in 1828, founded a Committee of Tea Culture and instructed his district commissioners in company circulars to explore regions that, according to the findings of British botanists and geographers, fulfilled the requirements for planting tea. The attention of bio-prospectors and geological prospectors soon focused on Assam because the mountainous border region of the annexed territory seemed suitable for laying out tea plantations.[2] Botanical exploration at first concentrated on the area between Assam and Burma in the north-eastern Naga Hills. As early as 1823 the brothers Robert (died 1824) and Charles Alexander Bruce (1793–1871) had observed tea plants growing wild and being harvested for local consumption. They failed to back up their observations with scientific evidence, however, because the botanical specimens they had collected near Rangpur (in what is now Bangladesh) could not be unequivocally identified by specialists at the Botanic Gardens in Calcutta (now Kolkata) as genuine tea plants (*Camellia sinensis*).[3]

Charles Bruce's report preyed on Captain Francis Jenkins' (1793–1866) mind: Jenkins, the district commissioner for Assam, was an amateur botanist. During his military campaigns in Assam, he had collected numerous plants and sent them to the Royal Botanic

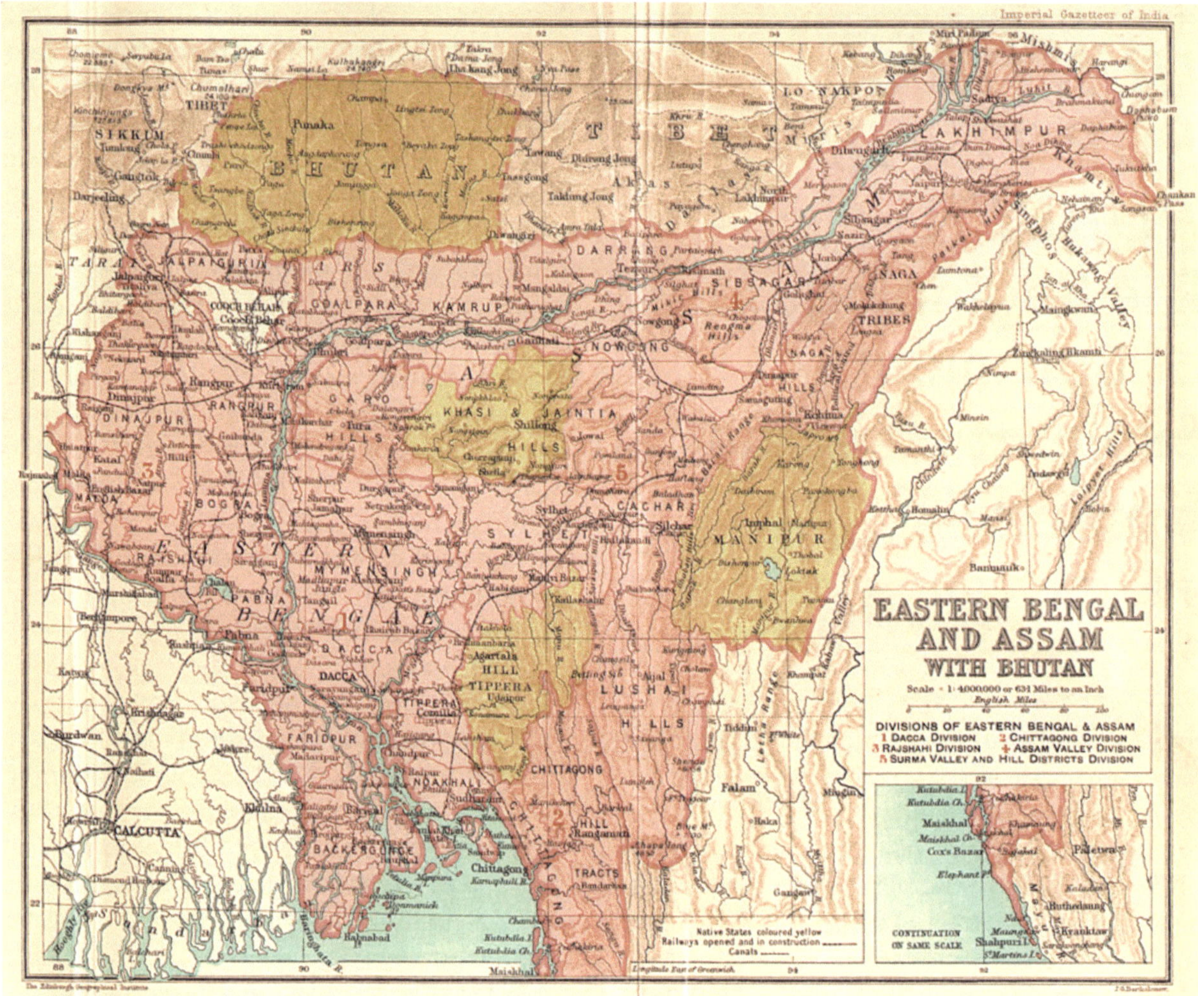

Garden in the London suburb of Kew.[4] In spring 1834, Jenkins went to the north-eastern tip of the district to look for wild tea plants in the hills around the border town of Sadyia. This time the experts in Calcutta confirmed that the specimens were indeed genuine tea plants, as Jenkins reported to his superior in an exultant letter on the findings 'that the tea shrub is beyond all doubt indigenous in Upper Assam. ... We have no hesitation in declaring this discovery ..., to be by far the most important and valuable that has ever been made in matters connected with the agricultural or commercial resources of this Empire.'[5] ——

On receiving the good news, the Committee of Tea Culture dispatched a distinguished European expert to study the region more closely from the botanical standpoint and assess its suitability for tea planting. Nathaniel Wallich (1786–1854), a Danish botanist employed by the botanical gardens in Calcutta and secretary of the Committee of Tea Culture, reached the tea forests near Sadyia in November 1835, accompanied by John McClelland und William Griffith (1810–1845), both doctors with a substantial knowledge of botany.[6] Although McClelland soon left the group, Wallich and Griffith succeeded in amassing a collection of some 1,500 plants within a surprisingly short timespan. The two bioprospectors were not just interested in luxury foodstuffs for the export market, viable agricultural crops, rare woods and medicinal herbs, but also in discovering new magnolia, primula and fern species to adorn English gardens.[7] In his final report for the Committee, Wallich strongly advised against cultivating the native wild tea plant from those forests and as an alternative sug-

Fig. 2 J. G. Bartholomew, Eastern Bengal and Assam with Bhutan. In *Imperial Gazetteer of India*, New edition, published under the authority of His Majesty's Secretary of State for India in Council Vol. 11, inside back cover.

gested importing tea shrubs and seedlings from China and cultivating them at trial plantations in northern Assam. The task was first undertaken by Charles Bruce. In founding the Assam Company in 1839, John White Masters (1791–1873), who had long worked for Wallich as head gardener in Calcutta, became overseer of the tea plantations for several years.[8]

After leaving that posting, Masters settled near Sibsagar in the upper Assam Valley to devote himself to botanical studies. When a military expedition set off in January 1844 to map the Naga Hills south of Sibsagar between the Rovers Dikho and Dhunsiri, Masters did not hesitate to join it. The expeditionary force was heavily armed but, driven by strong monsoon rains and a nagging fear of attack, traversed the region quickly,[9] leaving Masters with little time for observing and collecting botanical specimens. He wrote in his report: 'Could I remain with safety on these hills for three or four years, I doubt not but I should reap a good harvest, but hurrying over them in the manner we were compelled to do, very little could be done in examining the Flora. I presume it would occupy an experienced Botanist 10 years to explore the whole of the Naga Hills in a satisfactory manner; none of them having been hitherto visited by any Botanist.'[10]

By the time the expedition ended after two months, the collections amassed by the retired plantation manager included some five hundred plant species, a list of which Masters published that year in the *Journal of the Asiatic Society of Bengal*.

In the 1830s, British army expeditionary forces engaged in what were known to be punitive expeditions in the Naga Hills, after Naga groups who feared the colonial power would invade their territories, had attacked workers in the tea plantations. Numerous reports written by military personnel in this connection and published in specialist journals did contain descriptions of individual plants and their uses without, however, systematically studying them.[11] That is why the list John White Masters published in 1844 of all plants he had collected in the Naga Hills can be viewed as the first purely botanical specialist publication in this field.[12] Apart from the scientific take on botany, Masters, as a former tea plantation manager and gardener, always kept the economic value of plants in mind. Three years later, he took part in another military expedition, this time to the Angami Hills, where he collected some 2,000 plant specimens. The report he subsequently made in 1848 to the Royal Horticultural Society of India did not resemble a checklist but, on the contrary, mainly emphasised new species that were edible, provided valuable woods and dyestuffs or were suitable for cultivation as decorative garden and house plants.[13]

Masters was, however, not the first European scholar to collect plants in the Naga Hills. The oldest herbarium specimens from the Naga Hills kept in European herbaria came from another protégé of Nathaniel Wallich's associated with the botanical gardens in Calcutta and mentioned above: William Griffith, an assistant surgeon employed by the East India Company, was a talented young amateur botanist who corresponded with many distinguished plant scientists of his day. It is hardly surprising, therefore, that Commissioner Jenkins recruited him for a second expedition after his exploration of the tea forests of Sadyia. This expedition also aimed at finding raw plant materials in the little-explored border regions of Assam. The prime object was this time the Indian rubber tree (*Ficus elastica*), whose milky white sap looked promising as a viable alternative to the latex tapped from the South American rubber tree (*Hevea brasiliensis*).[14] Griffith was commissioned by the London Caoutchouc Company to observe the local inhabitants extracting the milky sap from rubber trees growing in the wild and send samples to London. Accompanied by a military escort, Griffith travelled in 1836–37 through the Mishmee (Mishmi) Hills north of Sadyia and then turned south-westwards to the Khasyia (Khasi) Hills.[15] During this expedition Griffith was the first European botanist to cross the Naga Hills, advancing to altitudes of up to 1,900 metres. Since this stage of his journey took place in March, a time of year unfavourable for collecting plants at high altitudes, not many botanical specimens found their way into Griffith's collection.[16]

It took a decade for the collection to be systematically evaluated. Griffith died young at thirty-five, leaving the work unfinished. Part of his estate comprising thousands of herbal specimens as well as ten folio volumes of botanical descriptions, travel notes and measurement data went to the herbarium at the Royal Botanic Garden in Kew.[17] Many items of information were lost: 'It is unfortunate that these fine herbaria should have been distributed promiscuously, without any determinate plan, and without any reference to his published notes and journals, which robs the collections of half their value, and the journals of more than half of theirs,' noted Joseph Dalton Hooker (1817–1911), who ultimately worked up Griffith's specimens scientifically, and in 1855 published *Flora indica*, the first systematic survey of the vegetation of Assam in general and the Naga Hills in particular.[18]

J. D. Hooker was the son of William Jackson Hooker, director of the Royal Botanic Garden in Kew, and succeeded his father as director in 1865. Hooker, who systematically studied the habitats of plant species while comparing the vegetation of different regions, is regarded as the founder of the discipline of geobotany. Like most nineteenth-century botanists, Hooker travelled extensively while still young, but devoted his later years to comparing his travel notes and herbarium samples with those amassed by other collectors and working them up as the basis for publications. Accompanied by a travelling companion, Thomas Thomson (1817–1878), Hooker undertook an extensive Himalaya expedition to Nepal, Sikkim and Tibet between 1847 and 1851, they became the first European botanists to do so. On their return journey through the Assam floodplain, the two botanists collected specimens in the mountainous regions of Sadyia and Khasyia (Khasi) but did not go to the Naga Hills.

In *Flora indica* Hooker's evaluation of the vegetation endemic to the Naga Hills was not, therefore, based on personal observation, but drew on scant herbarium specimens, travel notes and publications by Griffith and Masters. As his point of reference, Hooker used the flora of the Khasyia (Khasi) Hills west of the Naga Hills because these hills were easily accessible via a traffic artery linking Silhet and Gowahatti (Gauhati) and were for this reason well represented in his herbarium with specimens amassed by several collectors. Besides Jenkins, Wallich/Griffith and Hooker/Thomson, professional plant hunters collected samples of living plants and seeds in Khasyia for export. One of them, Thomas Lobb,[19] was commissioned in 1849 by Veitch, a large nursery in Exeter, to scour the region for orchids, for which the English aristocracy was willing to pay a fortune so they could show the exotics off in their glass houses.

'The Naga hills, to the eastward, probably exhibit a very similar vegetation to the Khasia, as their elevation is about the same. ... The flora of the Naga hills is only known by the few notes published in Griffith's journals, as the collections which he made there have not been distributed. Except *Liquidambar* and *Kaulfussia assamica*, Griffith notes no plants as differing from those of the Khasia; the general forms are therefore certainly the same. He especially alludes to the absence of Coniferae, of which however a species is said to abound on the hills of Manipour, to the southward.'[20]

Hooker's pronouncement on the vegetation of the Naga Hills marked the high point and the temporary end of early botanical exploration of them because he was the most distinguished botanist of the day and his word was hardly challenged at all in the years that followed. Most travellers preferred in any case to bypass the foothills and advance into Himalayan regions at higher altitudes. Thus, when botanical specimens happened to be collected on the way to them, as they were by the brothers Hermann Schlagintweit (1826–1882) and Robert Schlagintweit (1833–1885), whose expedition in 1854–1858 was a joint Prussian-British undertaking to explore India and Central Asia, they were found in the already thoroughly explored Khasyia (Khasi) Hills.[21]

Three decades would pass after Griffith's expeditions before another botanically trained collector would travel to the area where the

Naga settled: Samuel Edward Peal (1834–1897), who set out for the region in May 1868. Peal's travel diary also contained numerous sketches and descriptions of plants;[22] nonetheless, no sharp botanical focus is apparent in the reports he published of his expedition, apart from a detailed description of a plant whose seeds were used to stupefy fish.[23] Peal was also the first plant collector to attempt direct barter with the inhabitants of the region. Collecting plants usually took place in the slipstream of heavily armed military escorts. Such conditions were hardly conducive to personal interaction and the exchange of knowledge between European scientists and local populations, and indeed the sources cited here show no evidence to the contrary.

The Naga Hills and the abutting hill regions were not the focus of botanical attention in the early phase of colonial occupation. However, the practices and exponents of a profoundly utilitarian colonial system based on extraction and maximising profits that consistently studied and exploited its plant resources by means of a well-organised network of botanic gardens are starkly revealed as if under a magnifying glass. Whether those involved were military men well versed in botany, plant hunters dabbling in botany as a side-line or trained plant scientists who willingly put their expertise at the disposal of the committee responsible for raw materials – their interests remain ambivalently placed between scientific curiosity and blatant striving for profits.

1 Sharma 2011, pp. 27f.

2 Ibid., pp. 29f.

3 Robinson 1841, p. 136.

4 Hooker 1855, p. 232.

5 Committee of Tea Culture 1835, p. 42.

6 Robinson 1841, pp. 138f.

7 Arnold 2008, p. 91.

8 Desmond 1994, p. 2069; Robinson 1841, pp. 138f; Sharma 2011.

9 Brodie 1845, p. 843.

10 Masters 1844, p. 708.

11 Grange 1839; Grange 1840.

12 Masters 1844.

13 Masters 1848.

14 Grotz/Rahemipour 2019.

15 Anonymous 1847; Griffith 1836; Griffith 1837; Griffith 1838.

16 Hooker 1855, p. 239.

17 Anonymous 1847.

18 Hooker 1855, p. 259.

19 Ibid., p. 268.

20 Ibid., pp. 239f.

21 Schlagintweit 1890.

22 See the essay by Roland Platz in this book.

23 Peal 1872, p. 31.

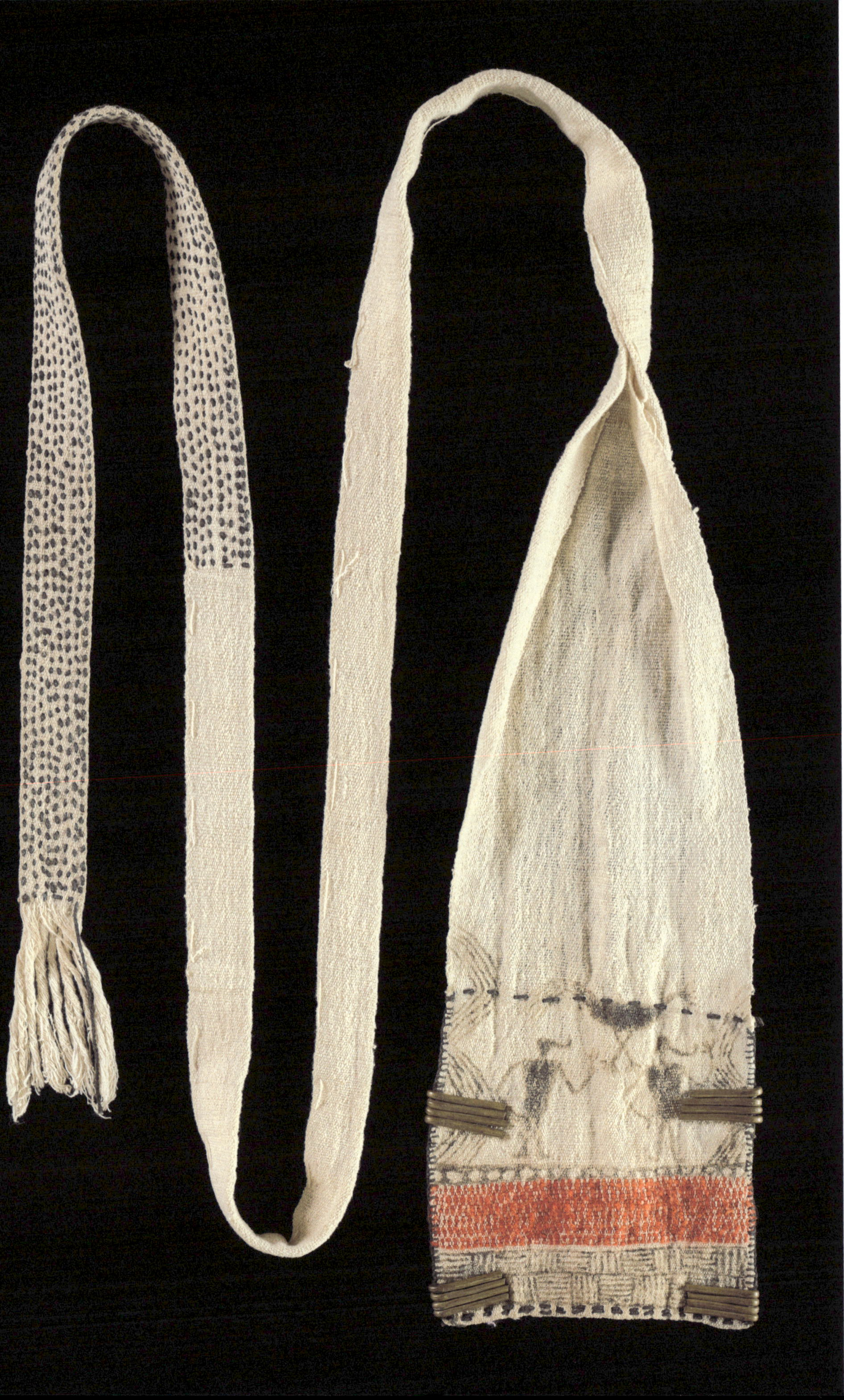

APPENDIX

Fig. 3: Loincloth *(langtum)*, Ao Naga, Nagaland, 2nd half 19th century, cotton fabric with design woven of red wool, painting and brass clips

Otto E. Ehlers Collection, donated in 1896 to the Royal Museum for Ethnology, Inv. No. I C28382, Staatliche Museen zu Berlin, Ethnologisches Museum

Hartmut Dorgerloh has been the general director and chairman of the board of the Humboldt Forum Foundation in the Berlin Palace since 2018. From 2002 until 2018, he was general director of the Stiftung Preussische Schlösser und Gärten Berlin-Brandenburg (Prussian Palaces and Gardens Foundation). An art historian and cultural manager, he has also taught at the Humboldt-Universität zu Berlin as an honorary professor since 2004.

Kathrin Grotz has been deputy director of the Institute for Museum Research at the Staatliche Museen Berlin since 2020. Previously, she was exhibitions manager and head curator at the Botanical Museum Berlin for many years. Apart from innovative formats for conveying knowledge, evaluation and visitor research, her area of expertise comprises natural history collections and the movement of objects within them.

Theyiesinuo Keditsu is an Indigenous feminist, poet, academic, folklorist, writer and educator. She has published two books of poetry and contributed to a number of anthologies and journals in her creative and academic capacities. She advocates for the revival of Indigenous Naga textiles and women's narratives through her popular Instagram avatar @mekhalamama. Keditsu has a PhD in cultural studies from the Tata Institute of Social Sciences, Mumbai. She is widely sought after as a public speaker in areas of literature, folklore, textiles, sustainable fashion, Indigenous feminisms and gender equity within her Naga community and in northeast India. She has over sixteen years of teaching experience and is currently an assistant professor in Kohima College, Kohima, Nagaland.

Dolly Kikon is a Naga anthropologist. She belongs to the Lotha Naga tribe from Nagaland. She teaches at the University of Melbourne. To follow her work, check out her website: www.dollykikon.com.

Lars-Christian Koch is director of the collections of the Staatliche Museen zu Berlin im Humboldt Forum (Berlin State Museums in the Humboldt Forum). An ethnomusicologist and ethnologist, he teaches ethnomusicology at the University of Cologne as an extraordinary professor, and as an honorary professor at the Berlin University of the Arts.

Aküm Longchari works in the areas of conflict transformation, peacebuilding, nonviolence, self-determination, decolonization and human rights. Since 1994, Aküm has been involved in grassroots peoples' movements. He is the cofounder and publisher of *The Morung Express* (2005), an independent English-language newspaper in Nagaland. He volunteers with the Forum for Naga Reconciliation.

Zubeni Lotha is a photographer from Nagaland. Her main focus of work is Nagaland, where the questions of representation and image making is explored. She is also the cocurator for the Naga exhibition at the Humboldt Forum, Berlin, in 2022. At present, she is the cofounder of (PINE) Peace Initiative in Northeast, a first of its kind for promoting a culture of peace in the northeastern region of India at the institutional level. She has developed a course of reading conflict with a special focus on photography, which she is currently teaching at a university in Dimapur.

Iris Odyuo is an associate professor at the Department of History at Sao Chang College in Tuensang, Nagaland, India. She is also a painter. She completed her PhD in history with a dissertation titled *A Study of Naga Artisans and Their Crafts: Continuity and Change* from the Department of History and Archaeology of Nagaland University, Kohima, in 2014. Her research focuses on Naga arts and artisanal production in the past and the present. She recently authored "Naga Art and Its Market through Time: Delocalization, State Control and Globalisation" in *Geographies of Difference: Exploration in Northeast Indian Studies* (coedited by Melanie Vandenhelsken, Meenaxi Barkataki-Ruscheweyh, and Bengt G. Karlsson).

Roland Platz is curator of the South- and Southeast Asian Collection at the Ethnological Museum in Berlin. He received his PhD in anthropology from Freiburg University. His research interests are identity studies related to ethnic minorities and historical photography. He has conducted fieldwork in northern Thailand and Nagaland. He was a lecturer at the Freiburg and St Gallen Universities and has worked as an intercultural communications consultant.

Elisabeth Seyerl-Langkamp studied Cultural and Social Anthropology as well as Theatre, Film and Media studies in Vienna and Ljubljana. She currently is a research associate in the Collections Department of the Humboldt Forum Foundation. She was part of the curatorial team of two exhibitions that deal with the historical collections of the Ethnologisches Museum Berlin. Previously employed there, she has also worked at the Weltmuseum Wien and the Dallas Museum of Art. Her research interest lies with textiles and fashion in ethnological museum collections.

BIBLIOGRAPHY

Abboud, R.W. *South American Backstrap Loom: Its Potential, Limitation and Application for Contemporary Handweaving*. University of Rhode Island 1975, Open Access Master's Theses, Paper 771, https://digitalcommons.uri.edu/theses/771 (20 Mar 2021).

Anonymous. 'Biographical Memoir of the late William Griffith', *Madras Journal of Literature and Science* 14 (1847): 187–97.

Arnold, D. 'Plant Capitalism and Company Science: The Indian Career of Nathaniel Wallich', *Modern Asian Studies* 42, no. 5 (2008): 899–928, www.jstor.org/stable/20488047 (13 June 2021).

Banerjee, R. 'Championing the Sartorial Value of Traditional Textiles: Theyiesinuo Keditsu', *Verve Magazine* online, 14 October 2019, https://www.vervemagazine.in/people/championing-the-sartorial-value-of-traditional-textiles-theyiesinuo-keditsu (12 July 2021).

Baruah, S. 'Confronting Constructionism: Ending India's Naga War', *Journal of Peace Research* 40, no. 3 (2003): 321–38.

Bastian, A. 'Hügelstämme Assam's' (lecture), *Verhandlungen der Berliner Gesellschaft für Anthropologie, Ethnologie und Urgeschichte, Zeitschrift für Ethnologie* 13 (1881): 149–60.

Bastian, A. *Völkerstämme am Brahmaputra*. Paderborn, (1883) 2011.

Bhuyan, G. 'North-Eastern Peeps Always Have the Best Sense of Style: A Case Study', in: *iDiva* online, 18 November 2019, https://www.idiva.com/fashion/trends/why-north-easterners-always-have-the-best-sense-of-style/18004402 (19 July 2021).

Brodie, T. 'Narrative of a Tour Over That Part of the Naga Hills Lying Between the Diko and Dyang River', *Journal of the Asiatic Society of Bengal* 14, no. 2 (1845): 828–44.

Burman, J. J. R. 'Contours of the Naga Upsurge', *Asia Europe Journal* 6, no. 1 (2008): 145–56.

Chingmak, W. *The Chang Nagas: In Memory of Our Undefeated Ancestors*. Dimapur, 2020.

Chishi, H. 'Myanmar Kids Maids in Nagaland', *The Telegraph* online, 5 April 2012, https://www.telegraphindia.com/north-east/myanmar-kids-maids-in-nagaland/cid/433783 (18 July 2022).

Clifford, J. 'Museum Realisms: What Does Realism Mean in Museum Contexts, Especially Those Concerned with Cross Cultural Translation?' YouTube video, 10 May 2016, Museum Volkenkunde Research Center for Material Culture, Leiden (20 March 2021).

Committee of Tea Culture. 'Discovery of the Genuine Tea Plant in Upper Assam', *Journal of the Asiatic Society of Bengal* 4, nos. 37–48 (1835): 42–49.

Crosby, A. W. *Ecological Imperialism: The Biological Expansion of Europe*. Cambridge, UK, 2004.

Danspeckgruber, W. (ed.). *The Self-Determination of Peoples: Community, Nation, and State in an Interdependent World*. London, 2002.

Das, N. K. 'Naga Peace Parleys: Sociological Reflections and a Plea for Pragmatism', *Economic and Political Weekly* 46, no. 25 (2011): 70–77.

Daskon, C. D. 'Cultural Resilience – The Roles of Cultural Traditions in Sustaining Rural Livelihoods: A Case Study from Rural Kandyan Villages in Central Sri Lanka', *Sustainability* 2, no. 4 (2010): 1080–1100.

Desmond, R. *Dictionary of British and Irish botanists and horticulturalists*. London, 1994.

Dirks, N. B. *Castes of Mind: Colonialism and the Making of Modern India*. Princeton, NJ, 2001.

Drouyer, I. A. *The Nagas: Memories of Headhunters: Indo-Burmese Borderlands*, Vol. 1. Bangkok, 2016.

Ehlers, O. E. *An indischen Fürstenhöfen*. Berlin, 1894.

Exotic Echo, International Loinloom Festival website, https://www.exoticecho.org.

Franke, M. *War and Nationalism in South Asia: The Indian State and the Nagas*. London/New York, 2009.

Freire, P. *Pedagogy of the Oppressed*. New York, (1970, 1993) 2000.

Fürer-Haimendorf, C. v. *Die nackten Nagas: Dreizehn Monate unter Kopfjägern Indiens*. Leipzig, 1939.

Ghosh, S. 'The Pangti Story: How a Nagaland Village Turned from Hunting Ground to Safe Haven for Amur Falcon', *Scroll.in*, 28 May 2018, https://scroll.in/article/877928/.

Graburn, N. 'Weirs in the River of Time: The Development of Historical Consciousness among Canadian Inuit', *Museum Anthropology* 22, no. 1 (2008): 18–32, https://doi.org/10.1525/mua.1998.22.1.18.

Grange, E. R. 'Extracts from the Narrative of an Expedition into the Naga Territory of Assam', *Journal of the Asiatic Society of Bengal* 8, nos. 85–96 (1839): 445–70.

Grange, E. R. 'Extracts from a Journal of an Expedition into the Naga Hills on the Assam Frontier', *Journal of the Asiatic Society of Bengal* 9, nos. 103–108 (1840): 947–66.

Gray, A. 'The British in Nagaland – Their Anthropology and their Legacy', in *The Naga Nation and Iits Struggle Against Genocide*, International Work Group for Indigenous Affairs (IWGIA). Copenhagen, 1986.

Griffith, W. 'Remarks on a Collection of Plants, Made at Sadiyá, Upper Assam, from April to September 1836', *Journal of the Asiatic Society of Bengal* 5, nos. 49–60 (1836): 806–13.

Griffith, W. 'Journal of a Visit to the Mishmee Hills in Assam', *Journal of the Asiatic Society of Bengal* 6, nos. 61–66 (1837): 326–41.

Griffith, W. 'Report on the Caoutchouc Tree of Assam Made at the Request of Captain Jenkins, Agent to the Governor General', *Journal of the Asiatic Society of Bengal* 7, nos. 73–78 (1838): 132–42.

Grotz, K. and P. Rahemipour. 'Pflanze Ikone Phänomen – Der Gummibaum', in Grotz, K. and P. Rahemipour (eds.), Geliebt Gegossen Vergessen. Phänomen Zimmerpflanze. Berlin, 2019: 112–17.

Heirloom Naga, business website, http://www.heirloomnaga.com/.

Hooker, J. D. *Flora indica: Being a Systematic Account of the Plants of British India, Together with Observations on the Structure and Affinities of Their Natural Orders and Genera*. London, 1855.

Iralu, E. 'Why Are Indians so Preoccupied with What Nagas Eat, Whether It Is Dogs, Bats or Falcons?', *Scroll.in*, 22 February 2021, https://scroll.in/magazine/987259/.

Jacobs, J. *The Nagas: Hill Peoples of Northeast India*. London, 2012.

Jamir, A. Instagram Account, Oslü Clothing Co., https://www.instagram.com/otsuclothingco/?hl=de.

Johnson, C. 'A Captured Nation: The Naga Dilemma', in *The Naga Nation and Its Struggle Against Genocide*, International Work Group for Indigenous Affairs (IWGIA). Copenhagen, 1986.

Joshi, V. 'Dynamics of Warp and Weft: Contemporary Trends in Naga Textiles and the Naga Collection at the Pitt Rivers Museum, Oxford', in Textile Society of America (ed.), *Approaching Textiles*,

Varying Viewpoints: Proceedings of the Seventh Biennial Symposium of the Textile Society of America. Santa Fe, NM, 2000.

Kikon, D. 'Cultural Construction of Nationalism: Myths, Legends and Memories', in Michael Oppitz et al. (eds.), *https://we-share.degruyter.com/index.php/f/1166169*, pp. 97–104.

Kikon, D. 'The Predicament of Justice. Fifty Years of Armed Forces Special Power Act in India', *Contemporary South Asia* 17, no. 3 (2009): 271–282, http://dx.doi.org/10.1080/09584930903108937.

Kikon, D. *Life and Dignity: Women's Testimonies of Sexual Violence in Dimapur (Nagaland)*. Guwahati, 2015.

Kikon, D. 'From the Heart to the Plate: Dog Meat Debate in Dimapur', *International Institute for Asian Studies* (2017), http://hdl.handle.net/11343/198142.

Kikon, D. *Living with Oil and Coal: Resource Politics and Militarization in Northeast India*. Seattle, WA, 2019.

Kikon, D. and B. G. Karlsson. *Leaving the Land: Indigenous Migration and Affective Labour in India*. Cambridge, UK, 2019.

Klemm, K. and S. E. Peal. 'Ein Ausflug nach Banpara: Nach der Original-Handschrift übersetzt und mit einer Einleitung versehen', *Zeitschrift für Ethnologie* 30 (1898): 281–371.

Kunz, R. and J. Vibha (eds.). *Naga: Eine vergessene Bergregion neu entdeckt*, Museum der Kulturen Basel. Basel, 2008.

Kunz, R. and J. Vibha (eds.): *Naga: A Forgotten Mountain Region Rediscovered*, Museum der Kulturen Basel. Basel, 2008.

Linn, A. J., J. D. Reuther, C. B. Wooley, S. J. Shirar, J. S. Rogers (eds.). 'Museum Cultural Collections: Pathways to the Preservation of Traditional and Scientific Knowledge', *Arctic Science* 3, no. 3 (2017): 618–34, https://doi.org/10.1139/as-2017-0001.

Longchari, A. *Self Determination: A Resource for Just Peace*. Dimapur, 2016.

Lotha, Z. Interview conducted by F. Schmidt, https://www.preussischer-kulturbesitz.de/newsroom/dossiers-und-nachrichten/dossiers/dossier-magazin-internationale-kooperationen/auf-der-suche-nach-identitaet-die-naga-ausstellung-im-humboldt-forum.html.

Macfarlane, A. and M. Turin. 'The Digitization of Naga Collections in the West and the Return of Culture', in Michael Oppitz et al. (eds.), *Naga Identities: Changing Local Cultures in the Northeast of India*. Gent, 2008.

Masters, J. W. 'Observations on the Flora of the Naga Hills, by Mr. J. W. Masters, Communicated by the Government of India to Captain T. Brodie, Principal Assistant Commissioner of Assam', *Journal of the Asiatic Society of Bengal* 13, nos. 151–156 (1844): 707–34.

Masters, J. W., Extract From a Memoir of Some of the Natural Productions of the Angami Naga Hills, and Other Parts of Upper Assam', *Journal of the Asiatic Society of Bengal* 17 (1848): 57–59.

Mazrui, A. A. *Cultural Forces in World Politics*. Oxford, 1990.

Mongro, K. *Naga Cultural Attires and Musical Instruments*, A. L. Ao (ed.). New Delhi, 1999.

Morung Express. 'HC directs Nagaland Government to Re-examine Honorarium for VGs', 8 February 2021, http://morungexpress.com.

Nagaland Post. 'Open Sale of Hornbill Bird dDspite Ban', 30 November 2018, www.nagalandpost.com.

Nuh, V. K. and W. Lasuh (eds.). *The Naga Chronicle*. New Delhi, 2002.

Odyuo, I. 'Naga Basketry with Special Reference to the Chang and Khiamniungan Nagas', in Michael Oppitz et al. (eds.), *Naga Identitie:. Changing Local Cultures in the Northeast of India*. Gent, 2008.

Odyuo, I. *A Study of the Naga Artisans and Their Crafts: Continuity and Change*. Unpublished PhD Dissertation Nagaland University, 2012.

Odyuo, I. 'The Various Aspects of Naga Art', *IOSR Journal of Humanities and Social Science* 9, no. 4 (2013): 13–22.

Oppitz, M., T. Kaiser, A. v. Stockhausen, M. Wettstein. 'Die Naga: Eine Einführung', in Michael Oppitz et al. (ed.), *Naga Identities: Changing Local Cultures in the Northeast of India*. Gent, 2008.

Peal, S. E. 'Short Notes of a Trip into the Hills South of Sibsugor; by A. C. Peel [sic], Esq. Communicated through Dr. J. Anderson, by Dr. Stoliczka', *Proceedings of the Asiatic Society of Bengal* (1869): 76–79.

Peal, S. E. 'Notes of a Visit to the Tribes Inhabiting the Hills South of Sibsagar, Asam', *Journal of the Asiatic Society of Bengal* 41 (1872): 9–31.

Phanjoubam, P. *The Northeast Question, Conflicts and Frontiers*. New York, 2016.

Ramunny, M. *The World of Nagas*. New Delhi, 1988.

Robinson, W. *A Descriptive Account of Asam, with a Sketch of the Local Geography and a Concise History of the Tea-plant of Asam: To Which is Added a Short Account of the Neighbouring Tribes, Exhibiting Their History, Manners, and Customs: Illustrated with Four Maps, Drawn Expressly for the Work* Calcutta/London, 1841.

Schlagintweit, E. 'Schlagintweit', *Allgemeine Deutsche Biographie*, vol. 31 (1890), pp. 336–48, https://de.wikisource.org/w/index.php?title=ADB:Schlagintweit&oldid=-.

Schneckenburger, S. 'Auf der Jagd nach dem "Grünen Gold": Botanische Gärten in der Zeit des Kolonialimus', *Biologie Unserer Zeit* 6, no. 40 (2010): 2–10, DOI:10.1002/biuz.201010435.

Sellato, B. 'Material Cultural Studies and Ethnocultural Identity', in V. T. King et al. (eds.), *Borneo Studies in History, Society and Culture*, Asia in Transition 4. Singapore, 2017, www.researchgate.net.

Sharma, J. *Empire's Garden: Assam and the Making of India*. Durham/London, 2011.

Shimray, A. A. S. *Let Freedom Ring: Story of Naga Nationalism*. New Delhi, 2005.

Sitlhou, M. 'How Covid Encouraged India to Shop Second-hand', *Vogue Business*, 12 February 2021, https://www.voguebusiness.com/sustainability/how-covid-19-encouraged-india-to-shop-secondhand.

Temsulong. 'Asenla Jamir from Nagaland Chats About Her Fashion Journey and Also Catch Her in the Upcoming Movie *Axone* by Nicholas Kharghongar', *Roots & Leisure* online, 18 September 2019, https://rootsandleisure.com/asenla-jamir-fashion-stylist-singer-actor-assam/.

Tetseo, K. Naganess blog, http://www.naganess.com/.

West, A. *Museums, Colonialism and Identity: A History of Naga Collections in Britain*. London, 2011.

Wettstein, M. 'Fashion Zeitgeist in Northeast India', in Tereza Kuldova (ed.), *Fashion India: Spectacular Capitalism*. Oslo, 2013.

Wettstein, M. 'The Ethnic Fashion Scene in Nagaland', *Archiv 61-62, in: Archiv Weltmuseum Wien, ed. by Verein Weltmuseum Wien Friends*, Vienna, 2013, pp. 31–50.

Wettstein, M. *Naga Textiles: Design, Technique, Meaning and Effect of a Local Craft Tradition in Northeast India*. Stuttgart, 2014.

Wohlforth, W. and T. Felgenhauer. 'Self-Determination and the Stability of the Russian Federation', in Wolfgang Danspeckgruber (ed.), *The Self-Determination of Peoples: Community,*

Nation, and State in an Interdependent World. London, 2002.

Wouters, J. J. P. 'Who Is a Naga village? The Naga Village Republic Through the Ages', in Jelle J. P. Wouters and Michael Heneise (eds.), *Nagas in the 21st Century*. Kohima, 2017.

IMAGE CREDITS

Cover and back cover:
© Zubeni Lotha

pp. 8, 10, 11:
© Staatliche Museen zu Berlin, Ethnologisches Museum. Photo: Martin Franken

pp. 12, 14, 15, 17, 18, 19, 20:
© Zubeni Lotha

p. 21:
© Staatliche Museen zu Berlin, Ethnologisches Museum

p. 22 above:
© Staatliche Museen zu Berlin, Ethnologisches Museum

p. 22 below:
© Staatliche Museen zu Berlin, Ethnologisches Museum. Photo: Annette Hlawa (reproduction)

p. 24:
© Staatliche Museen zu Berlin, Ethnologisches Museum. Photo: Martin Franken

pp. 26 and 27:
© Aküm Longchari

p. 28:
© Staatliche Museen zu Berlin, Ethnologisches Museum. Photo: Martin Franken

p. 30 above:
© Staatliche Museen zu Berlin, Ethnologisches Museum. Photo: Martin Franken

p. 30 below:
© Iris Odyuo, photo: Alban von Stockhausen

p. 32:
© Staatliche Museen zu Berlin, Ethnologisches Museum. Photo: Martin Franken

p. 33:
© Iris Odyuo

p. 34:
© Staatliche Museen zu Berlin, Ethnologisches Museum. Photo: Claudia Obrocki

p. 36:
© Iris Odyuo. Photo: Alban von Stockhausen

p. 37:
© Staatliche Museen zu Berlin, Ethnologisches Museum. Photo: Martin Franken

pp. 38 and 39:
© Iris Odyuo

pp. 41, 42, 44–47, 51:
© Staatliche Museen zu Berlin, Ethnologisches Museum. Photo: Martin Franken

pp. 52, 54, 56:
© Dolly Kikon

pp. 57,58, 60, 62–64, 68, 70:
© Staatliche Museen zu Berlin, Ethnologisches Museum. Photo: Martin Franken

pp. 72–74:
© Theyie Keditsu

p. 75:
© Arsenla Jamir

p. 77:
© Staatliche Museen zu Berlin, Ethnologisches Museum. Photo: Martin Franken

p. 78:
© copyright of the Board of Trustees of the Royal Botanic Gardens, Kew

p. 80:
© Digital South Asia Library

p. 84:
© Staatliche Museen zu Berlin, Ethnologisches Museum. Photo: Martin Franken

COLOPHON

Published by the Stiftung Humboldt Forum im Berliner Schloss

This book is published in connection with the exhibition ***NAGA LAND: VOICES FROM NORTH-EAST INDIA*** at the Humboldt Forum Berlin, 2022–2023

An exhibition by the Stiftung Humboldt Forum im Berliner Schloss in cooperation with the Ethnologisches Museum and the Museum für Asiatische Kunst in the Staatliche Museen zu Berlin – Preußischer Kulturbesitz, the artist and curator Zubeni Lotha from Nagaland and the Botanischer Garten and Botanisches Museum Berlin

Exhibition curatorial team:
Zubeni Lotha, Roland Platz, Kathrin Grotz, Elisabeth Seyerl-Langkamp, Barbara Lenz

Exhibition project team:
Noelle von Galen, Frauke Gathof, Johanna Kapp, Nadine Ney, Friedrun Portele-Anyangbe, Johanna Scherer, Leonie Seitz, Maike Voelkel, Constanze Wicke

Head of exhibition department:
Anke Daemgen

The Stiftung Humboldt Forum sincerely thanks for their professional assistance and support: The curators, the authors, the lenders, Luxoom Medienprojekte GmbH, Imchatsung Imchen, Amit Mahanti, Mira Dallige-Smith, Kerstin Flemming, Martin Franken, Thomas Kaiser, Lars Krutak, Mo Naga, Tanja Milewsky, Claudia Obrocki.

We are also grateful to the staff of the Stiftung Humboldt Forum im Berliner Schloss, the Ethnologisches Museum and the Museum für Asiatische Kunst in the Staatliche Museen zu Berlin and all those not named here who contributed to the success of this project.

Publication project direction:
Roland Platz

Concept:
Nadine Ney, Roland Platz, Elisabeth Seyerl-Langkamp

Editorial staff:
Susanne Müller-Wolff, Roland Platz, Johanna Scherer

Picture editing:
Barbara Martinkat, Roland Platz

www.humboldtforum.org

Supported by the Federal Government Commissioner for Culture and the Media according to a resolution of the German Federal Parliament

The Deutsche Nationalbibliothek lists this publication in the Deutsche Nationalbibliografie; detailed bibliographic data are available on the Internet at http://dnb.dnb.de.

Publishing:
Deutscher Kunstverlag GmbH
Berlin München
Lützowstraße 33
10785 Berlin
www.deutscherkunstverlag.de

Part of Walter de Gruyter GmbH
Berlin Boston
www.degruyter.com

Project management:
Luzie Diekmann
(Deutscher Kunstverlag)

Production management:
Jens Lindenhain
(Deutscher Kunstverlag)

Translation from German into English:
Joan Clough

Copyediting: Aaron Bogart

Layout and typesetting:
e o t . Berlin

Image processing:
Bild1Druck GmbH, Berlin

Printing and binding:
Grafisches Centrum Cuno GmbH & Co. KG, Calbe (Saale)

Printed in Germany

ISBN 978-3-422-99080-7

Die Beauftragte der Bundesregierung für Kultur und Medien